The Simplicity
of the West

The Simplicity
of the West

by

Peter Milward SJ

The Saint Austin Press
1998

THE SAINT AUSTIN PRESS
296, Brockley Road,
London,
SE4 2RA.

© 1998, Peter Milward SJ

ISBN 1 901157 95 4

A catalogue record for this book is available from the British Library

Printed in Great Britain by BPC Wheatons, Exeter.

Cover: A Spanish Cloister, Estella (Navarre) (©Peter Milward)

Contents

Preface   7
1. Where is Wisdom?   11
2. The Master and His Disciples   17
3. Return to Nature   24
4. The Golden Age   32
5. The Lady Poverty   40
6. The Cloud of Unknowing   47
7. Under the Greenwood Tree   56
8. The Noble Savage   64
9. Behold the Child!   73
10. Renaissance of Wonder   81
11. Approach to Ecology   87

Preface

"Knowledge is power" is taken as a typical Baconian axiom. It is also taken as typical of the modern West, with all our advances in science (knowledge) and technology (power). And so we have achieved a society dominated by the male reason, much to the indignation of our modern feminists with their insistence on a return to nature. And not without reason do they insist. The more we pride ourselves on the domination of reason over nature, the more we find nature has its own way of taking revenge. "Expel nature with a pitchfork," the proverb reminds us, "yet it has a way of returning" – much to our chagrin. And so we have come to face the serious ecological problem, to which we turn in vain to scientific technology for an answer.

But then, is the above-mentioned axiom typical only of the modern West? The Baconians themselves appealed to the words ascribed to God himself at the very beginning of the Bible, where God blesses man saying, "Be fruitful, and multiply, and replenish the earth, and subdue it." There is no limit, it seems, to man's rights of subjugation over the earth. But is that what we find in the Bible? And if so, why did it take such a long time for men to discover its hidden implications – till the time of Sir Francis Bacon? Rather, what we find in the Bible is a preference of the countryside over the city, where even Jerusalem comes to seem rural in contrast to the great city of Babylon. For the divine choice rests on the poor of the earth, those who are outcast as exiles on the face of the earth, such a one as the virgin Mary in the village of Nazareth. And from her comes Jesus in his birth in the stable of Bethlehem, in his youth in the carpenter's workshop at Nazareth, in his mission among the towns and villages of Galilee, and in his death as an outcast beyond the city wall of Jerusalem. Such is the Christian ideal: of simplicity, poverty and exile – not of the knowledge that brings power.

And what of the Western world before the coming of Christianity? Here, too, we find an ideal of simplicity first among the Greeks, then among the Romans who came after. What is the inspiration of Socrates but the ideal of self-knowledge, which is very different from the knowledge of nature that brings power. For the true knowledge of self brings humility, the realization that all one can expect to know in face of the overwhelming power of nature is next to nothing. It is the realization echoed by Newton in modern times, when he confessed that in view of all that remained to be discovered in the world of nature he was but a little child playing on the seashore. In any case, the Athens of Socrates' time was but a village with walls; and outside those walls it was an easy walk into the surrounding countryside. There rational knowledge was deeply rooted in nature, however abstract its expression may seem to us today. And as the city grew, especially in Alexandria and later in Rome, there also grew a nostalgia or longing to return to the simple countryside, as expressed in the idyllic poems of Theocritus and Virgil.

Yet Virgil went on from his celebration of the countryside (and his native Mantua) in the *Eclogues* to his admiration for the urban ideal of *Roma Eterna* in the *Aeneid*. Similarly, when Christianity subsequently came to Rome with the apostles Peter and Paul, we find an interesting adaptation of Virgil's ideal to that of the eternal city, heavenly Jerusalem as celebrated in the end of the Bible, in the last two chapters of the Book of Revelation. And so Christianity came to flourish in the cities of the Roman Empire, leaving the countryfolk outside those cities with the name of *pagani*, at once rustic and heathen. All the same, once the Roman Empire was on the way to becoming Christianized under the Emperor Constantine, it soon appeared that the city was by no means the ideal place for Christian life in practice. And so we have the strange phenomenon of exodus from such cities as Alexandria, Antioch and Rome to the surrounding countryside and even desert – the phenomenon that is called "monasticism", or the life of a hermit in the desert. There alone, it seemed, could the ideal of Christian simplicity, poverty and suffering, be achieved, and not in the city. And so the Roman Empire tottered to its downfall, as recorded in the pages of Gibbon's *Decline and Fall*; while the barbarian nations of the North and West came to inherit the blessings of Christ.

Always, however, the city is reappearing among men, as before at Athens, Alexandria and Rome, so now at Paris and London, not to mention Florence, Venice and another, Papal Rome. And always there is the opposite hankering after a primeval simplicity, both among the friars who are blessed by the Pope and among the later reformers who are cursed by him. For what is the meaning of the Reformation under Luther (among other things) but a rejection of the complexity of the mediaeval Church and a return to the pure simplicity of the Gospel of Christ? Yet such, paradoxically, was also the inspiration of his contemporary Ignatius of Loyola: a return to the Gospel message with the fresh eyes and ears of a child. And the outcome of all this reform, whether rejected by the Church (in the case of Luther) or accepted (in the case of Ignatius), what was it? With the increasing abandonment of tradition and accumulation of riches from the newly found lands in America and Asia, we find a corresponding secularization of culture and development of scientific knowledge that has come to its climax in our own day. And can we say this climax is good or beneficial to mankind? All we can say is that, like the fruit of the original tree of knowledge in the Garden of Eden, it is at once good and evil. With this knowledge we find we can do all kinds of things, including the destruction of ourselves; and this latter we are now in process of doing!

What then? Must we reject all knowledge and all culture, like the frenzied followers of Pol Pot in Cambodia? Or must we turn at least from the civilization of the West which has cultivated this knowledge that brings power, and return to the simpler civilizations of the East, at least as they used to be before the incursion of the West with its consequent corruption – as seen notably in modern Japan? But there is no need to turn from the one civilization or return to the others, in blind ignorance of the one and the others. What is needed is a return at once to nature, in which all true civilization whether West or East has its root, and to tradition, in which the natural roots of civilization may be seen to flourish and develop from generation to generation. This is precisely what I propose to show in the present book: to show the true ideal of "the simplicity of the West", as it has developed and flourished from age to age, for all the various periods of corruption which are incidental to human development. After all, as Aristotle pointed out, "the corruption of one thing is the generation of another" – and even its own regeneration. For it is important to know the true development of a culture so rich as that of the West, if only to profit from the mistakes of the past without repeating them. This is true revolution: not to reject the past and to begin anew – like Shakespeare's Laertes, "as the world were now but to begin, antiquity forgot, custom not known" – but to receive from the past (as St. Paul recommends) "whatever is true, whatever is modest, whatever is just, whatever is holy, whatever is loveable, whatever is highly regarded, whatever is virtuous and worthy of praise". In other words, what is needed is a revolution like that of springtime in nature, in which the old is made new again and the past is made present – according to the ideal of Christ himself as stated at the end of the Book of Revelation: "Behold, I make all things new!"

1. Where is Wisdom?

Two (among many) characteristics of our modern world are the ever-increasing complexity of human life and the ever-decreasing awareness of human history. These two characteristics, especially as I have just phrased them, are no mere chance phenomena of the modern scene but closely inter-connected. The rise of the one (complexity) almost necessarily entails the decline of the other (awareness of history). This may even be said of modern historical science, seen as one among the many disciplines in the academic world. With all the emphasis laid on precise historical knowledge, on the careful ascertaining of facts and the meticulous documentation of sources, something essential is overlooked; and that is an understanding of those facts as parts in the light of a greater whole – of the facts as trees in relation to the forest in which they have their setting. And with that understanding, looking beneath the outward complexity to an inner simplicity, comes wisdom.

For history is a fascinating subject when approached in this manner, in a human manner. It is so much more than an assemblage of facts, to be memorized and tabulated for a merely academic purpose. It does not consist merely in facts or events, still less in the documents recording those facts or events, but rather in the human beings involved in them. It is essential to remember that history is made by human beings like ourselves, and that we, too, as human beings, are involved in those facts and events, even when they took place in an age and at a place far removed from ourselves in the twentieth-century. After all, as the Roman dramatist Terence remarked in one of his plays, we are human, and nothing of human interest ought to be indifferent to us. That is the very motto of humanism!

Such, for example, was the approach of Shakespeare to English history in a series of no less than ten plays from the reign of King John to that of King Henry VIII. He was, of course, a dramatist, not a professional historian; but he took certain chronicles of English history and interpreted them in a human, dramatic manner, with a certain measure of his own imagination. For imagination, even creative imagination, is necessary to enter into the minds of human beings and to interpret the mere facts of history. And so he succeeded in making English history fascinating to the members of his Elizabethan audiences. So, too, with Sir Walter Scott, the romantic novelist, who was one of the first authors to popularize the genre of historical novel with his series of "Waverley novels". He took various historical events, whether from the old Middle Ages in *Ivanhoe* or from his native Scotland in *Rob Roy*, and brought them to life as few scholars have succeeded in bringing them to life. And so he made mediaeval and Scottish history fascinating for generations of English readers from his day to our own. Scholars may despise such popular presentations of history; but they themselves, in most cases, derived from them their first taste for history.

But history is more than just bringing the past back to the living present, or setting present readers back in the dead past through an imaginative reconstruction. After all, there is so much whether in the past or the present that is tedious and even meaningless. I suppose the majority of events and conversations, however vividly recorded with a view to their human interest, are somewhat dull, remaining as they do on the surface of life; and so in our own experience we easily forget them. There is so much in life and experience that, for our own sanity, we have to forget. We can't remember everything, or we would become mad! In a way, forgetfulness is no less important to man than memory. So it is wittily said that true culture is what you remember when you have forgotten everything else.

History is, therefore, not just the presentation of facts and events, but the selection of significant facts and events. And how is one to judge their significance, without some interpretation? All too often the interpretation is left in the

12

hands of snobs, who have an eye only for "very important persons", such as Hideyoshi in Japanese history or Winston Churchill in Western history, men who seem to command the destinies of nations. I don't deny that historical events, such as the Japanese invasion of Korea in the sixteenth century and our own World War II, have to be explained with reference to such great men. But in the study and interpretation of history, we have to consider not only what they did or decided or failed to do, but also why they did so, what moved them as human beings, and what inspired them. Then, by asking the all-important question "Why?", we pass beyond or beneath the level of mere outward appearances to that of inward human reality. It is precisely the concern of a dramatist like Shakespeare or a novelist like Scott, to look to the inner motives and the characters of those human beings who "strut and fret" on the stage of human history.

This is also what John Henry Newman points out in his *Idea of a University*, as the true purpose of university education – a purpose which, I regret to say, is almost entirely forgotten in most universities of Japan and (I venture to add) of the West. In most universities, both here and abroad, students and their teachers are engaged in a pursuit of knowledge whether of the natural world or of human history and behaviour. But how few of them raise their eyes from their books or their experiments to ask themselves about the basic meaning of what they are studying? What is the point of knowing about the natural world or about the past and present deeds and thoughts of other men? What is the profit of knowing all these things, if the knower doesn't really know himself or his own place in the world? It all comes down to the basic words of Jesus Christ to his followers, "What does it profit a man, if he gain the whole world (by such knowledge as brings power) and suffer the loss of his own self (or his own life)?"

It is precisely such a question, as Newman wisely points out, that leads the questioner from the mere level of knowledge – knowledge of facts and events, of human beings and their motives – to the deeper level of wisdom. And it is in this question, or rather in following it (as far as we can) to some kind of an answer, or what Graham Greene calls "the hint of an explanation", that we come upon the true purpose of university education, which is not knowledge but wisdom. Of course, not any answer will do. One answer, for instance, is that there is no answer; but that is a hopeless, a desperate answer, like the cynical remark of George Bernard Shaw, "The golden rule is that there is no golden rule." Nor may we expect to find the answer by asking an eminent scholar, who may have spent his life on the mere level of knowledge and never dreamt of passing beyond to the level of wisdom. "What is wisdom?" he may contemptuously ask, in much the same tone as Pontius Pilate when he asked Jesus, "What is truth?" Nor may we expect to find the answer in a simple statement, which may mean much to the speaker but little to his listener. Rather, everyone has to find the answer for himself; and for each person it may well take a different form of words, or thoughts – though it is really deeper than any form of words or thoughts. What is more, for everyone it takes a whole lifetime of patient, humble, persevering inquiry; and when he finds it, he finds it not only here or there, but everywhere.

Such, for example, is the question we find recurring in the pages of the Old Testament, rather than in university lectures or scholarly, books: "Where is wisdom to be found?" It comes in the Book of Job, in the Book of Psalms; in the Book of Proverbs; it is, in short, the typical question of the so-called sapiential books of the Bible. And what is the answer given to this question? It is a very simple one; for knowledge is various and complicated but wisdom is simple. It is all put in a nutshell in all the above-mentioned passages, which all repeat that at least the beginning of wisdom is "the fear of the Lord". You may, of course, say, "Easier said than done." But I would rather say, "Easier said than understood." To understand these seemingly simple words may well take a lifetime, even to reach the starting-point. But as I see it, in the beginning is already an implication of the end; for if the beginning of wisdom is fear, the end is surely love, the love of the Lord. And that, too, is "easier said than understood".

But now let me turn from the Old Testament to the New, and from the so-called law of fear to the other law of love. In the time of Jesus there were many teachers or exponents of the law of Moses, who were called "the scribes". From the way they are described in the gospels, they would seem to correspond to what I have said of pedantic scholars today, who make learning seem so difficult. In their interpretation of the law, they made it seem so difficult in the eyes of ordinary people; and so Jesus criticized them for binding heavy burdens and laying them on men's shoulders. By contrast, he showed the Kingdom of God as a place not for scholars or rulers, not for the wise or the powerful, but for children and poor people, for the simple and even (or especially) the foolish. For, as St. Paul later said, it is the foolish and the weak of this world God has chosen to confound the wise and the powerful. For such people, who would never dream of going to a university, or who would never be admitted into any university, the way to wisdom is open, a way leading straight from the fear to the love of God.

Again, let me turn from the Bible to the Classics, and to the figure in the Classics of Greece who most resembles Jesus. I mean Socrates. He, too, gathered a group of disciples round him, and he, too, stood out in opposition to the professional teachers of his time, the so-called "sophists". By asking them a series of questions, according to his method of "irony", by assuming an air of ignorance, he showed that they weren't really as wise as they pretended to be – by leading them to contradict themselves. His aim wasn't, of course, to annoy them but to make them think about the true nature of wisdom; but in

15

fact he did annoy them by pricking the bubble of their empty reputation for wisdom. And in their anger they accused him of atheism and so brought him to death; just as the scribes and other leaders of the Jews in their anger accused Jesus of blasphemy and so brought him to his death on the cross.

The moral of all this may best be stated in a motto that concerns not so much the teaching of Jesus or Socrates as that of Confucius: *"Rongo yomi no rongo shirazu"* – "It is precisely the professional scholars of the Analects who do not understand the Analects". It is the danger, as we say in English, of not seeing the wood, or the forest, for the trees. A person may be so immersed in the details of what he is studying, whether law or literature or science, that he is unable to see it as a whole. He is like one who stands right in front of a famous painting, poring over each detail, but never thinks of standing back to appreciate the painting as a whole – the way paintings, and all works of art and literature, have to be appreciated. This is the very definition of wisdom given by the great theologian. St. Thomas Aquinas, who considers knowledge as divided or scattered among many things and wisdom as uniting those many things in one idea. And all things on earth he sees as united in heaven, in the goodness and love of God.

2. The Master and His Disciples

One of the first books I read in Japanese, while I was studying at the language school after my arrival in Japan, was a novel about Shinran entitled *The Priest and His Disciples*. I forget the name of the author, but the title he chose for his novel was, I thought, a very impressive one. And it seemed to me a very suitable title not only for his story of Shinran, but also for the gospel of Jesus. What I liked about it was the implication that the teaching of the master Shinran wasn't just a one-way traffic or communication, from above to below, with the master preaching long sermons and his disciples humbly listening to his words of wisdom. It was rather a two-way traffic or conversation, with the master still teaching, of course – otherwise, he could hardly be called "master" – but his disciples responding with questions and answers. It is what is called nowadays "feedback", with the master providing "input".

Anyhow, that is just what we find in the four gospels that present the teaching of Jesus Christ. They are not really sacred books written in an ancient, liturgical language, to be solemnly intoned in a mystic chant which may be impressive but which few people can understand. They may have been used by monks for this purpose, but that isn't why they were originally written. From the beginning in the first century A.D., they were written down in the ordinary language of the time, in what is called *koinë* or common Greek (in contrast to classical Greek), for ordinary people to read; as the authors themselves, disciples of Jesus (Matthew and John) or at least disciples of those disciples (Mark and Luke), were ordinary people. What they set down were their personal memories of Jesus, not only his words but also his deeds and his sufferings, as well as his personal relationship with them. Naturally, they include some of his sermons, such as the famous sermon on the mount, so far as they can remember the words; but for the most part the gospels read like a prolonged conversation between Jesus and his disciples. And the implication is that this conversation doesn't just end with the last chapter of the gospels, but that it is continued from generation to generation of disciples until the end of time.

What is more, this is a very natural conversation. It is carried on not within a church or (to speak in terms of Jesus' time) a synagogue. Occasionally Jesus may speak in a synagogue on the Sabbath day, and occasionally we are told what he said there; but more often than not the synagogue is the setting for the working of a miracle of healing. Anyhow, there is no special emphasis on the synagogue; but the setting of Jesus' words and deeds is more often a natural one, on the hillside, by the roadside, or by the sea he prefers (it seems) to live and speak and converse with his disciples outside, in the open air; and when he prays, usually at night, when he has more free time, he likes to go up a hill or a mountain. Or if he remains indoors and speaks with his disciples there, it is more often than not in the setting of a meal. Unlike his ascetic precursor, John the Baptist, Jesus seems to be fond of eating and drinking, admittedly not so much for the actual food and drink as for the opportunity of conversation in a natural, relaxed mood. One might even say, Jesus is nothing if not natural and for him the natural is precisely the way to the supernatural.

Here, then, is the ideal of Christian education. Here is the true "idea of a university", as expounded in later years by John Henry Newman. It has little to do with buildings or classrooms, with professors or tutors, least of all with a complicated administration – all those bureaucratic details of which government officials are so fond. No, it is a personal relationship between the master and his few disciples, whose number is limited to twelve, according to "the twelve tribes of Israel". It is a relationship that consists not just in daily instruction, as it were a series of lectures or sermons, but much more in daily life and intercourse. Jesus

18

himself even compares it to the relationship between bridegroom and bride, or at least between bridegroom and friends of the bridegroom, leading up to the bridal feast or wedding reception which is realized at the last supper. In the course of this relationship, there is, of course, a training or education imparted by the master; but this is not so much an intellectual formation, such as that provided by Socrates in classical Greece, as a personal formation based on a deepening faith and love. The faith is not only faith in God as Father, but also faith in Jesus as Son of God; and the love is, similarly, not only love of God above all things, but also love of Jesus in himself and in all men.

All the same, there has to be some message, something which Jesus wishes to tell his disciples. And, of course, there is such a message. It is what Jesus wishes by all means to tell his disciples; but for some reason, though it may be simple in itself, it isn't so easy for him to communicate to them by word of mouth. What is felt very deeply in the heart isn't always easy to put into words. It is rather the opposite: what is easily put into words is probably not felt so deeply in the heart. Such was the case with the three daughters of King Lear. The two who loved him least were the ones who could most easily express their "love" in fluent words; but the one, Cordelia, who loved him most found she could only say "Nothing". Or even if Jesus had put into words what he most wanted to tell his disciples, as (for instance) that "God is love", they wouldn't have understood him. So he had to prepare their minds gradually, to lead their minds onwards and upwards till they were ready to accept what he had to tell them. Here, in fact, may well have been one of his greatest and most personal problems: how to tell his disciples what he most wanted to tell them.

To understand what Jesus most wanted to say, we have to go back to the beginning of what is called his "public life", his baptism by John at the river Jordan. Though himself without sin, he wished to receive baptism as a symbol of repentance, if only to show his unity with sinful men and to lead them from their old ways to a new way of life. Then it was that he heard a voice from heaven saying, "This is my beloved son, in whom I am well pleased." What was the meaning of this mysterious voice? Clearly, it was an encouraging, comforting voice from heaven, the voice of God as Father, speaking to Jesus as Son, the object of his divine love. It was a voice coming down to Jesus in the present from the remote past, from the prophecy of Isaiah, where we find much the same words addressed to a mysterious servant. Now it seems, Jesus is identified as that servant, only now he is called "Son"; and in him are placed the hopes of Israel, as he is to fulfil all that is prophesied concerning that servant, otherwise known as the Messiah, the Christ, the anointed Saviour of his people. But still there is a mystery in the voice, and in the words uttered by the voice; and so, we read in the gospel, Jesus is impelled by the Spirit to withdraw into the desert of Judea, no doubt to reflect on the mysterious significance of the voice.

Here I would like to emphasize two ideas that are also deep in Japanese tradition, that of *mu* or "nothing", and that of *ku* or emptiness – two Chinese characters that originally came (I am told) from the same Sanskrit word. First, in his baptism Jesus takes off his clothes to go into the water, symbolically putting off his former life at home in Nazareth and setting forth on a new life, concerning which he has no idea. For him everything is in God's hands; and he has nothing of his own, he has emptied himself of everything. So now be goes into the desert, where there is nothing, where all he can do is fast and pray. And he has presumably no idea of what lies before him, beyond leaving everything in God's hands. Only, he has the voice from heaven still ringing in his ears, and the question, what does it mean for him? Obviously, it means that God is his Father and he is the Son of God in a relationship of love; and that is not just the beginning but already (as I have said) the end of wisdom.But it also implies a mission among men, and a

20

message to communicate to them. Once he has heard it, it is easy enough for him to receive it and to reflect on it here in the desert. But how to communicate it to other men, how to assure other men that they, too, are loved by God, that as God is Father they, too, are called to be sons of God – that is the problem facing him, especially once he leaves the desert and returns to the company of men.

It is enough for him to go and tell them, "God loves you. God is your dear Father. You are called to be sons and daughters of God." Of course, he can say this in so many words; but will they believe what he says? Won't they think he is just an idle dreamer, he is too childish? Won't they laugh at him, instead of listening to him? Rather if he is to get them to hear the voice from heaven, he must first lead them as it were into the desert as Moses had first led the people of Israel from the land of Egypt into the desert, there to meet God at Mount Sinai. He must first get them to leave their old ways and their possessions and preoccupations, so that they may put on a new way of life, according to the symbolism of water and the spirit. He must preach to them the ideal of poverty, which is the ideal of the kingdom of heaven, not of earth.

Such are, in fact, the first words of Jesus to the people in his opening sermon on the mount. After going round repeating the words of John, "Repent, for the kingdom of God is at hand", Jesus begins his sermon on the mount by saying, "Blessed are you poor, for yours is the kingdom of heaven." How astonishing! He begins by congratulating his hearers on their real poverty, which already introduces them to the ideal kingdom of heaven. Ile wants them to see their poverty with new eyes, he wants them to appreciate their poverty fhich-makes them no less familiar with heaven than with earth. By their poverty they are close to earth, if they are farmers, tillers of the soil, or close to water, if they are fishermen in the nearby lake; and by their same poverty they are also close to the angels of God in heaven, they are themselves sons of God, if they will only accept the

21

heavenly invitation. By their poverty they seem to have nothing, deprived of all earthly goods; but in fact, if they will but open their eyes and see the truth, they have everything. The earth is theirs, the water is theirs, the air around them, the sun, the moon and the stars in the sky, all is theirs, if only they appreciate it all and thank God for it all Not the richest man in the world has as much as they have, if they will only realize it, and if only they willingly embrace their poverty, if only they are (as we say) "poor in spirit". Rather, the possession of earthly riches is restricting: it makes a man a slave to his greed. It is poverty that is liberating, introducing a man to his true inheritance, extending upwards from earth to heaven.

This is why Jesus himself follows the way of poverty in his public life, saying, "The foxes have their holes, but the son of man has nowhere to lay his head." This is why he goes on to invite his disciples to follow the same way of life, to give up all things and to come after him. As he said to the rich young man who sought a more perfect way of life, "If you would be perfect, go and sell all you have and give it to the poor, then come and follow me." It is also a way of simplicity, doing without all except what is necessary for keeping body and soul together; and for that purpose, so little is really necessary, as Jesus had found for himself during his forty days of fasting and prayer in the desert. It is also a way that is close to nature, close to the flowers of the field and the birds of the air, and close to the loving providence of our heavenly Father. It is also a way of childhood, as Jesus said to his disciples, "Unless you are converted and become as little children, you cannot enter the Kingdom of heaven." Or rather, it is a way not only of childhood, but also of rebirth as little babies, by which we address God not only as "Father", but also and more particularly (as Jesus himself often prayed to his Father) as "abba!", that is, "papa!", "baba!" in the first utterance of an infant.

This is, in short, the wisdom that Jesus wishes to teach

his disciples, as he has already learnt it from the heavenly voice of his Father. It is a wisdom towards which he has to lead them gradually by getting them to experience a life of poverty with himself, a life of simplicity and closeness to nature. He has to lead them from the natural pride and ambition of adults, by the way of childhood, to a condition of humility and acceptance of nothing; and that is, in reality, the way of the cross. So he also says to his disciples, "If any man would come after me, let him deny himself and take up his cross daily and follow me." Here, too, he leads the way, showing his disciples what it means in bitter reality to take up the cross and carry it to the hill of Calvary for his eventual crucifixion and death. For that is what it means to become nothing, to be emptied of oneself, in this world: not just a silent, passive contemplation of the void, but an agony of pain and persecution, rejected by the world. And even in the beginning of his public life in his sermon on the mount, Jesus proceeds from his blessing on the poor to his further blessing on the persecuted, so long as they accept their sufferings for the kingdom of heaven

3. Return to Nature

Turning from the Bible to the Classics, and from Israel to Greece, we may note the remarkable similarity in life and character between Jesus and Socrates. Each of them is, of course, unique in his several setting; but the uniqueness somehow serves to underline the similarity. Each of them bore witness to the truth, as he saw it; each of them gathered a group of disciples round him; each of them taught in the form rather of friendly conversation, often while eating and drinking, than of a lecture or sermon; each of them was tried on a false charge, made by professional enemies, and sentenced to death. Neither of them wrote any treatise, whether of ethics or of religion; but their memory was kept alive by their disciples and their words were set down in the form whether of gospels or of dialogues. And so what Jesus is to the Christian Church, Socrates is, in a less formal, organized manner, to Greek philosophy. Only whereas Jesus still lives and the Church he founded still thrives, Socrates has largely been forgotten, except by students of the Classics and in textbooks of world history.

Anyhow, the influence of Socrates is great on the philosophical tradition of the West, especially as it is traced back to his disciple, Plato, and to Plato's disciple, Aristotle. To begin with Plato, it is all but impossible to distinguish or divide the ideas of Plato from those of his master Socrates, for the simple reason that the ideas of the former, as presented in his dialogues, are invariably put into the mouth of the latter. Socrates (like Moses) is as though in the place of God, and Plato (like Aaron) is as it were his prophet. Or (to vary the metaphor, in terms of the New Testament), if Socrates is like Jesus, Plato is like the beloved disciple John, parts of whose gospel are strangely reminiscent of Plato's *Phaedo*, which gives the last dialogue of Socrates and his disciples before his death. But the characteristic ideas of Plato, especially his so-called "theory of ideas", are challenged, disputed and refuted by his own disciple Aristotle – in a pattern that becomes all too typical of Western education. And Aristotle goes on to present his thought in the more systematic form of lectures, rather than dialogues. So if Plato may be said to have founded the ideal of "academy", Aristotle was rather the founder of the other ideal of "university".

There is, however, a notable difference (one among many) between this line of Greek philosophers and Jesus with his disciples in Galilee. And that is the difference in setting between the city and the countryside. For Socrates, Plato and Aristotle, the setting is the city of Athens, which Millton in his *Paradise Regained* presents as the fourth, his own additional, temptation of Jesus in the desert. In the background of their philosophical ruminations we may see the splendid architectural structures of the Acropolis, culminating in that wonder of the ancient civilized world, the Parthenon. But for Jesus and his disciples, the setting is the countryside of Galilee, with the flowers of the field growing on the hillside overlooking the lake, and the birds of the air flying and singing over that hillside and the lake. Thus the former are closer to the works of man, collectively known as "civilization"– while the latter are closer to that work of God which is called "nature".

But there is, of course, more to the world of classical Greece than the philosophy of Socrates, Plato and Aristotle, however central their thought may seem in the intellectual tradition of the West. There were other philosophers before, during and especially after this famous trio, who represent a reaction against the increasing urbanization and civilization of human life and a return to the origins of that life in the world of nature. Such a philosopher was the contemporary of Aristotle and Aristotle's great pupil, Alexander the Great, the founder of the school of "cynics" (a name derived from "dogs"), Diogenes. In his disgust with the civilized world of man, he took off his clothes and lived in rags, he abandoned his house and dwelt in a barrel. Once he visited Plato in the latter's mansion and, trampling on the carpets with his dirty feet, he exclaimed, "Thus do I trample on the pride of Plato." (To which Plato responded, "But with other pride!") On another occasion, he was visited by the great Alexander, who graciously asked him if he lacked anything in his barrel. "Yes," answered Diogenes, with studied rudeness, "You are standing in my light!" Subsequently in Shakespearian drama we may find a disciple of Diogenes in the tragedy of *King Lear*, in the person of the banished Edgar, who is driven to such a desperate condition by the wicked plot of his ambitious brother Edmund. Yet in him the mad Lear recognizes the true condition of man in this fallen world: "Is man no more than this? Consider him well. Thou owest the worm no silk, the beast no hide, the sheep no wool, the cat no perfume . . . Thou art the thing itself. Unaccommodated man is no more but such a poor, bare, forked animal as thou art." And so he seeks to learn from Edgar as his "Theban" or "Athenian" philosopher.

In such individual, even idiotic philosophers and their disciples we may find a pattern strangely similar to that of Jesus and his disciples, who were also in their time regarded as idiotic, estranged from the civilized world of normal men and women. Even the relatives of Jesus are said (by Mark) to have regarded him as "out of his mind"; and other Jews are said (by John) to have despised him as "mad". Subsequently, Paul, too, in his letter to the Corinthians admits there are not many wise men among the disciples; but he explains that "God has chosen the foolish things of the world to confound the wise", and he even adds: "If any man among you seems to be wise in this world let him become a fool, that he may be wise."

Among the Greeks, Diogenes and his fellow Cynics weren't the only ones to turn away from the excessive urbanization and sophistication of the cities, and to return to a more natural, primitive, even naked way of life. The ideal of a "return to nature" was precisely that proposed by the Stoic philosophy, founded by Zeno of Citium at Athens a little after the time of Aristotle. Usually we think of the Stoics as grim-faced ascetics, who emphasized duty rather than pleasure as the moral imperative of human life. But this is an exaggeration, just as it is exaggerated to think of their opponents, the Epicureans, as advocating a life of sensual pleasure. Rather, what is characteristic of the Stoics is their emphasis on the "way of nature" as the way of reason and the way of the whole universe, governed as it is by the wisdom and the providence of God. So by "nature" they meant not so much the nature of plants and animals, or what we come across in the countryside, as the nature of man – what man should be, according to the ideal of reason, in contrast to what he is, all too often sunk into sensual vices.

If I may speak of myself and my student days for a moment, before I went up to Oxford for my study of classical literature, I spent three years in the countryside of Oxfordshire studying mediaeval philosophy. In the scholastic philosophy of the Middle Ages, what most impressed me, as it must impress anyone, is the predominant influence of the two Greek philosophers I have mentioned above, Plato and Aristotle. Plato was the formative influence on the great Christian theologian, St. Augustine; while Aristotle was chiefly taken up in the later mediaeval period by St. Thomas Aquinas and his followers. But when I went on to study the classical literature of Greece and especially Rome, I was surprised to find that neither of these great Greek philosophers had much influence on the literature of Rome. Orators like Cicero, poets like Lucretius, Virgil and Horace, seemed to be more interested in the ethical philosophy of the Stoics and/or the Epicureans. Lucretius was the great advocate of the Epicurean school; whereas his successor Virgil was no less ardent on the side of the Stoics. Cicero in his treatise on Duty, known as *The Offices*, refers not so much to Zeno as to later Stoic philosophers in Greece; and as for the more genial poet Horace, he speaks of himself as now a Stoic, now an Epicurean, as the mood seizes him. In fact, what I know of Stoic philosophy from original sources is chiefly what I came across in the writings of Horace. In his charming *Epistles* he speaks about the ideal of living in conformity with nature, of doing nothing to excess, of maintaining a rational equilibrium. But it is Cicero who actually uses the phrase, "follow nature", in his prose writings, and this is echoed by the English poet Alexander Pope in speaking of poetic composition. "First follow nature, and your judgment frame by her just standard, which is still the same."

Of course, this is not so much what we mean by physical nature in plants and animals, in the countryside apart from the city, as the rational ideal of human nature. But it considers human nature not just in itself, in man alone, as in the whole cosmic order of the universe. In fact, it seems to me that what the Stoics meant by nature comes very close to what the Chinese, both Taoist and Confucianist, meant by the Way. There is a certain order of things, under the wise supervision of divine providence, that is evident as well in the heavens above, in the movement of the stars, as in the earth below, in the succession of the seasons. Only, it is left to man by his use or abuse of his intellect and free will to take his proper part in this order or to disturb it by his wanton desires. In the countryside man is close to the order of nature on earth, and the succession of the seasons; and it is by keeping to this order that he is able to produce the fruits of the earth in due time and in abundance. But even in the city, so long as man follows the dictates of reason, according to the movement of the stars in heaven, he may still be close to the order of nature. All too often, however, in the city man becomes removed as well from nature on earth as from nature in heaven, as he yields to the temptations of material riches and political ambition. And these temptations were particularly felt in such cities as Alexandria in the Eastern Mediterranean and Rome to the West.

Now it was in reaction against such temptations in the two above-mentioned cities that there appears in classical literature a poetic version of the "return to nature". This was pastoral poetry, or a poetry that idealized the simple lives of shepherds and shepherdesses, in a mythical land called Arcadia. In Southern Greece there was indeed a land of that name, rustic, primitive and mountainous; but the poetry arose not out of that Greek countryside, but out of the busy, bustling city of Alexandria, from the pen of a poet named Theocritus. In such a setting, he was filled, as not a few dwellers in modern cities like London and Tokyo are filled, with nostalgia for "the good old days" when people lived for the most part in the simple countryside, scattered in farms and devoted to the tilling of the soil, or tending their flocks of sheep and goats up the mountainsides. Farmers, he reflected, would be more busy with their various tasks; but shepherds and shepherdesses would have plenty of time to indulge in such innocent pastimes as singing and love-making. And their songs in such an idyllic setting provided him with ample material for his poems, in which he appealed to the feelings of like-minded readers. Indeed, the very word he chose for his poems was "idylls", from which we have the adjective "idyllic" for the kind of life described in them.

Then from Greece and Alexandria (which was a later extension of Greece, from the time of its foundation by the great Alexander) there was a natural movement to Rome; since the Romans of old, like the Japanese of today, were great imitators of whatever they found in Greek culture and literature. So the idylls of Theocritus were taken up and adapted to the context of imperial Rome and the Latin language by Virgil, in his first major poems, the *Bucolics* or *Eclogues*. Whereas it was the boast of the emperor Augustus that he found Rome brick and left it marble, it was rather the dream of Virgil to get away from the city of Rome – much as he praised it in his subsequent epic, the *Aeneid* – into his native countryside near Mantua in North

Italy. Then, as though not content with his composition of ten pastoral poems, he went on to compose four further poems on farming, entitled the *Georgics* (*geōrgos* being the Greek word for farmer, and the origin of the English name of George). It is in these latter poems that he exclaims, "How extremely happy are the farmers, if only they realized their good fortune!" Much the same attitude one notices in Virgil's intimate friend Horace, though he never got down to composing pastoral poems. In one of his *Epodes* he also exclaims, "Happy the man who, far from busy cares, like the primitive race of men, ploughs with oxen his ancestral lands with no burden of usury on his neck!"

Needless to say, there are many other riches to be found in the abundant treasury of classical philosophy and literature than the few I have presented in this chapter. Yet, if I may again refer to my own studies at Oxford, I felt that this vein was by far the most interesting and congenial to my English temperament, however much the nature of the Mediteranean may differ from that of England. After all, just as human nature is basically the same everywhere, beneath differences of race and colour, so the natural countryside is much the same, allowing for differences of country and climate. What is more, it is, I think, this vein in classical philosophy and literature that was most congenial to the early Christians as they spread westwards from Israel by way of Greece and Alexandria to Rome. As the philosophy of Plato seemed to lend itself to the development of Christian theology in the writings of such great thinkers as Origen and Augustine, so the ethics of Stoicism seemed a kind of pagan precursor to the ethical teaching of Christ and St. Paul. As for the pastoral poetry of Theocritus and Virgil, it was taken up by later generations of Christian poets, especially in the Middle Ages and the Renaissance, when it seemed to flower again in a second spring; and Virgil himself, by virtue of one of his pastoral poems, the so-called Messianic Eclogue, came to be regarded as all but

Christian, and a saint of the classical pagan world.

4. The Golden Age

In speaking of classical literature and the ideal of a "return to nature", I left one important element of this ideal (among many) untouched. I mean the ideal of a "golden age" in a mythical, primitive past. Here by "golden" is meant not the actual possession and display of gold, such as one finds at an advanced stage of human culture, whether in the Babylon of Nebuchadnezzar or in the Rome of Augustus or in the Paris of Louis XIV "the Sun King" or in the Tokyo of today. Such an age of wealth and grandeur is rather characterized (according to this ideal) as an age of iron, in which the countryside has come to be despised and the city to be glorified. No, the "golden age" of the poets, such as Hesiod in Greece and Virgil in Rome, is a remote, primitive age, an age of poverty, simplicity and hospitality (three things that invariably go together), set in the countryside. It is an age when all the "gold" is in the hearts, not the pockets of men. It is an age when there is none of that "accursed thirst for gold" rejected by Virgil, none of that "love of money" which is for St. Paul "the root of all evils", but a simple contentment with the bare necessities of life such as we find expressed both by Stoic writers (such as Horace) and by authors of the Bible (from Solomon to St. Paul).

In the Bible the ideal of "the golden age" takes the particular form of Paradise, or the Garden of Eden, in which Adam and Eve were created by a loving God from the beginning. It is not so much a real as a mythical garden, or one might call it an allegorical garden such as that which features in the charming mediaeval allegory of love, *The Romance of the Rose*. It is an allegory of primitive happiness, innocence and love, before the fall of man and woman. In that garden state there is no money and no greed, only lovely plants and friendly animals as the setting of the ideal love between Adam and Eve, the ancestors of mankind. Only, there is a serpent and a tree of the knowledge of good and evil, symbolizing the temptation and the object of excessive desire. Whereas God has told man and woman, "If you eat the fruit of this tree, you will surely die," the serpent assures the woman "No, you will not die, you will become as gods knowing good and evil." And so she takes the fruit and eats it, and then she gives it to Adam, who also eats it; and so their eyes are opened, and tl,ey see themselves as naked; and so they are banished from the Garden of Eden into the wilderness of the outside world. They have lost their primitive innocence, and exchanged it for experience. They are driven into the outside world, where we are shown their sons, Cain and Abel, following an agricultural and pastoral life (respectively); but it is among the sons of Cain, notably Enoch, that the first city is said to be built.

Thereafter in the Old Testament we find a basic, but hidden, contrast between the sophistication of city life and the simplicity of the countryside. It is from the sophisticated culture of the Chaldeans that Abraham is called by God to "a promised land", where he goes and lives as a shepherd, though blessed with abundance of sheep and cattle. Then there is a division between him and his cousin Lot: he remains in the hills, while Lot chooses the luxurious life of the cities in the plain, the cities of Sodom and Gomorrah, subsequently destroyed by the wrath of the Lord. Later, when famine drives the sons of Israel into exile in Egypt, and they go on to multiply and thrive in that land, but then they find themselves oppressed by Pharaoh and the Egyptians, it is Moses who leads them out of the rich but oppressive land of Egypt, through the empty desert, back to the promised land of their fathers. There they remain for the most part a simple people of the countryside, devoted to an agricultural and pastoral life. At the most, they have a small capital city of Jerusalem, the city chosen by their king David both for his royal dwelling and for the temple of the Lord. In its smallness and comparative insignificance, it is contrasted with the great city of Babylon. In the course of time, Jerusalem with its holy temple is destroyed by the power of Babylon, under Nebuchadnezzar; but it remains as an ideal city, which is rebuilt from time to time, in contrast to Babylon, which is destroyed, never to be rebuilt. This is the contrast to which the whole of the Bible seems to lead up, in the Book of Revelation or Apocalypse, where the fall of Babylon (or Rome) precedes the manifestation of the heavenly city, the new Jerusalem.

In looking to this ideal city, however, I seem to have turned away from the primitive ideal of a "golden age" in the countryside. But we are speaking in terms of symbols; and symbolically speaking, there is at first a real contrast between the simplicity of the countryside and the sophistication of city life, as a contrast between good and evil; but as we turn our eyes from the real to the ideal, we find an ideal city, too, which is not opposed to the ideal of the country or the garden. Anyhow, in comparing the Greek and Roman Classics with the Bible, we may notice an interesting contrast: that whereas the classical writers for the most part look back to the primitive past for their ideal age, the Biblical writers look not so much to the ideal Garden of Eden in the past as to an equally ideal Messianic age and kingdom in the future. Thus in the classical writers, especially in the Roman poets, Virgil and Horace, we find an essential pessimism – though admittedly offset by the need to flatter the emperor Augustus; whereas what we find in the Biblical writers is an essential optimism. Yet the fomer aren't poor or miserable, but fairly well off, under the kindly patronage of Maecenas, the right-hand man of Augustus; and so his name has become proverbial for the generous patron of letters. It is the latter who are poor and miserable; and yet out of their poverty and misery, they raise their eyes in hope to the coming of the Messiah. And in the promises of their prophets, from Isaiah onwards, it is precisely among the poor that the Messiah is to come.

This is, moreover, precisely what we also find at the beginning of the New Testament. When Jesus is born, as we read in the Gospel according to Luke, it is in the reign of the emperor Augustus; and his birth in Bethlehem, the little city (or village) of David, is owing to a decree of that emperor, ordering the enrolment of all his subjects throughout the empire, each in his native region. So Mary and Joseph make their way from the village of Nazareth in Galilee to the town of Bethlehem in Judea, because Joseph belongs to the house and family of David; and there Jesus is born in poverty and laid in an animals' manger, "because there was no room for them in the inn". And the first people who come to adore him as their new-born king are not the rich and powerful from the city of Jerusalem, but poor shepherds with their sheep from the hills round Bethlehem, as though representing a traditionally pastoral people. Only afterwards are the gentile nations represented by the wise men from the East, who come according to the sign of the star.

It is in this setting of poverty and simplicity, of a stable or cave at Bethlehem, that the prophecy of Isaiah concerning the Messiah is fulfilled in the relationship between mother and child, Mary and Jesus. "A virgin shall conceive and bear a son," foretells Isaiah in one of the most important sentences of the Old Testament; "and he shall be called Emmanuel, God with us." And so, in the beginning of the New Testament, we are shown the virgin Mary conceiving by the word of the angel Gabriel and giving birth to her son Jesus, who is in reality God. As we read in the beginning of the Gospel according to John, "And the Word was made flesh, and dwelt among us." Interestingly enough, about the same time in Rome, we find the fulfilment of a similar prophecy in the words of the poet Virgil, in his above-mentioned Messianic Eclogue. Here he looks not only back to the "golden age", presided over by the Virgin Justice under the reign and star of Saturn, but also forwards to a fulfilment of prophecy that is already present, in the birth of a mysterious child (whose identity remains a matter of scholarly dispute) to his mother. He

35

even addresses the new-born child, "Begin, little son, with a smile to know your mother." Now the prophecy to which he refers is that of the Sybil, or old prophetess, at Cumae in the South of Italy; and it so happens that in the period between Alexander and Augustus there were many such prophecies (that have come down to us in Greek) emanating from the Middle East and evidently influenced by the original prophecy of Isaiah. So this eclogue of Virgil is more Messianic than he himself may have realized!

As for the further development of this prophecy in the life of Jesus, if he was born in poverty at Bethlehem and grew up in the simplicity and hardship of life as a village carpenter in Nazareth, it was in extreme suffering and utter destitution that he died on the cross outside the city of Jerusalem. Indeed, all his life we find a natural preference for the countryside and the lakeside of Galilee, and a corresponding reluctance to go up to the city of Jerusalem or the surrounding desert of Judea. So we might well expect that when his disciples went forth, at his command, into the outside world to preach the gospel to all nations, they would also show a similar preference of the countryside to the city. But no! It is the very opposite. From the beginning, after the final departure of Jesus into heaven, they remain for a time in Jerusalem, whose church continues to be regarded as the "mother church". And when they go forth as witnesses to Jesus "in Jerusalem, and in all Judea, in Samaria and to the utmost parts of the earth", we find them concentrating chiefly on the cities of that ancient world, Antioch in Syria, Ephesus in Asia Minor, Athens and Corinth in Greece, and eventually Rome. After all, it is in these cities, rather than in the surrounding countryside, that most people are to be found; and it is to people, rather than to plants or animals, that they are to preach the Gospel of Jesus, and to bear witness to his life, death and resurrection, as the light of salvation for all men. So we find Peter, as rock of the new Church and shepherd of the flock of Christ, leaving Jerusalem to establish headquarters first in the city of Antioch, then (by way of Corinth) to the city of Rome.

Not that the disciples are welcomed in the cities to which they go, not even in the Jewish communities or ghettoes where they naturally make their dwelling for a time. Rather, as we read in the *Acts of the Apostles,* they are persecuted by the Jewish authorities wherever they go, as heretics against Jewish orthodoxy; and then, ironically, they are persecuted by the Roman authorities together with the Jews. Such persecution was already foretold them by Jesus himself, when he warned them, "You will be persecuted by all men for my name's sake"; and yet in this way they win the blessing he also foretold them at the beginning of his sermon on the mount. Thus it is that Rome comes to replace Babylon as the symbolic "city of this world", in contrast to the "city of God", in the imagination of the disciples as expressed above all in the Book of Revelation attributed to St. John. Thus, ironically, it is at once the "eternal city" hailed by the poet Virgil in his *Aeneid* and the infernal "city of this world", ruled by the "prince of this world", the evil one, whose downfall is foretold by St. John under the figure of Babylon. "Alas, alas! Babylon the Great is fallen!"

In the early Church, it is true, the bishops all have their sees, or seats of rule, in the cities; and the bishops of such great cities as Rome, Antioch and Alexandria, that claim apostolic foundation, are also named patriarchs. By contrast, the people in the surrounding countryside, who cling to their traditional beliefs and customs and are not so easily converted to the new faith of Christianity, are known as "pagans" – which in the original meaning of the Latin word *paganus* refers to countrymen, rustics, even bumpkins. Yet once the persecutions came to an end in the early years of the fourth century A.D. and Christianity suddenly became the official religion of the Roman Empire under the rule of Constantine (though he didn't receive baptism till he came to die), we find an opposite movement, as though in accordance with the deep instinct of

Christianity. This is, needless to say, a movement from the city to the countryside; but this time, not the natural countryside, as an ideal Arcadia with trees and flowers beside flowing brooks and birds singing in the branches, but the wilderness of the desert in Egypt and Arabia, in Judea and Syria, and among the mountainous regions of Asia Minor, Greece and Italy. It is a movement away from the sinful life of the cities, which remain no less sinful in Christian times, to the ideal following of Christ in the surrounding wilderness, as monks and hermits.

True, the life of Jesus as recorded in the gospels is shown rather in the countryside of Galilee, in country towns and villages and by the wayside, than in the desert of Judea. But at least his first forty days and forty nights in that desert, when he is tempted by the devil, provide a pattern for these hermits who now come to people the above-mentioned deserts from the fourth century onwards. On the other hand, such a solitary life in the desert no more accords with the example of Jesus than life in the big cities, whether Babylon or Rome. And so as this ideal of "monasticism" moves from the Middle East, with its abundance of desert land, to the greener West, we find the solitary life of a hermit changing to the community life of a monk, especially under the rule established by St. Benedict in the sixth century A.D. The very name of "monk", whose original meaning in Greek is a solitary hermit, now comes to refer to a religious man living in a community of monks, or a monastery, under the rule of an "abbot" or father.

At first, these monasteries were established, as we see in the life of St. Benedict himself, away from cities like Rome and for the most part in the countryside. Yet it isn't long before we find a monastery even in Rome, and a monk being chosen even as Pope of Rome, the great St.Gregory I ; and it is from the nearby monastery of St. Andrew in Rome that this Pope sends Augustine (not the great theologian, who lived in Africa a couple of centuries before) and his companions to England. Thus already we see monks, so far from living as hermits alone in the desert, sent from the great city of Rome to preach the gospel to the people in England. There it was the principle of monks like Augustine to set up monasteries, such as the one he set up just outside the city walls of Canterbury, and from there to evangelize the people in the surrounding countryside. The ordinary priests and faithful in the Christian lands of the old Roman Empire, or what was left of it after the so-called "barbarian invasions", were too settled in their homes to be easily sent out as missionaries to pagan lands. But this was now the task of the monks, who had thus moved from the ideal of Christ in the desert to the further ideal of Christ in his public life of teaching in Galilee.

In this context, of the preaching of the gospel of Jesus Christ in England, we come upon an interesting confrontation of two forms of Christianity, or rather two forms of monasticism, the Roman and the Celtic. For while Augustine and his monks were engaged in spreading the Gospel both in the South and in the North of England, in the respective kingdoms of Kent and Northumbria, there were other monks from Ireland and Scotland spreading the same gospel in Northumbria. And while the Roman monks looked from the cities of Canterbury and York, as their headquarters in England, to the great city of Rome, the Celtic monks looked rather to their remote island monasteries in Lindisfarne (or Holy Island) and Iona in the Scottish Hebrides, and only vaguely to Ireland. This confrontation came to an issue at the Council of Whitby in 664, when the decision was given in favour of Rome. Yet somehow it has continued in the racial difference in the British Isles between the Celts on the one hand, who are more individualistic in temperament, and the Anglo-Saxons, followed by the Normans, on the other hand. Only, what united them, at least until the time of the Reformation, was their common Christian faith and their common Messianic ideal whether they saw this ideal in remote islands or in the central city of Rome.

5. The Lady Poverty

In order to understand the rise of Western culture, it is necessary to know something of what the historian Edward Gibbon has called "the decline and fall of the Roman Empire". It is what St. John had already foretold in his Book of Revelation, in terms of Babylon, "Babylon the Great has fallen!" Right up till the time of St. Augustine, the great Christian theologian, who lived and wrote in North Africa in the first half of the fifth century, men thought and spoke of Rome as "the eternal city", a city that, unlike other cities, would never fall. But then there took place a series of disasters known as "the barbarian invasions", first the Goths, then the Vandals, then the Huns, in successive waves; and so not only the city but also the empire, at least in the West, tottered and fell. And so the city was for a time replaced by the countryside and even the forest. Subsequently, in the seventh century the power of Islam appeared in the East, out of the desert of Arabia, and overwhelmed the lands of Syria and Mesopotamia, Egypt and Africa (that is, the Northern coast of what we call Africa), right into Spain and up to the Pyrenees. And so the centre of Western culture shifted from the Mediterranean to France and Germany and England; and the old Roman Empire was replaced by a new Holy Roman Empire, beginning with the solemn crowning of Charlemagne as Emperor by the Pope at Rome in the year 800.

These ages, both before and after that important date in Western history, are commonly known as "the dark ages". In some ways, they were no doubt dark, as the lives of men were spent under an almost continual threat of invasion, not only from Goths, Vandals and Huns, who were gradually converted to the gospel of peace, but also from Saracens and Vikings and Mongols; and it was only about the mid-eleventh century that these successive threats were eventually put aside. All the same, something precious was growing up in the Western nations during these troubled times, something simple, poor and primitive, something that entitles the period to be described as a "golden age". For it wasn't just the age of "the decline and fall of the Roman Empire", lamented by the classical author Edward Gibbon: it was also, and much more, "the rise of western culture", as set forth by the eminent modern historian, Christopher Dawson.

I myself recall with pleasure my introduction to what is called Old English or Anglo-Saxon literature at Oxford – when I passed in my studies from the Classics to English I had never read anything of this literature before, the literature that was written roughly from the seventh to the eleventh century in England, as it seemed to be written in a totally different language, more like German than modern English. But after studying something of its grammar and vocabulary, I came to read certain prescribed texts, centring on the anonymous eighth-century epic *Beowulf*, and I was deeply impressed. It wouldn't be too much to say that I had never come across any literature like it: it was so beautiful yet so powerful, so rich yet so primitive, so simple yet so profound.

It was also from the outset deeply Christian – from the time (shortly after the Council of Whitby and in the same place) the first English poet Caedmon composed his first poem on the creation. Then there was the lovely poem entitled "The Dream of the Rood", or the Cross of Christ, in which it is the Cross that speaks to the aged poet with words of sorrow and comfort. And after these poems comes the prose of the one great king of England, Alfred the Great, who may claim to be the founder of English prose, for the education of his kingdom.

Not many monuments remain from this period, apart from the literature, chiefly because the Anglo-Saxons built in wood, not stone; and whatever they built was improved upon (and thus destroyed) by the succeeding Normans, who had a passion for building castles and churches in stone. But for this very reason, it seems to me, they had the

41

true spirit of Christianity, which is closer to wood than to stone, closer to the countryside and the forest than to the city. After all, wood comes from the living tree and somehow remains alive even after the tree has been cut down; whereas stone is, by contrast, dead. Moreover, trees come from the earth's surface and so houses made of wood fit in with the landscape; whereas stone has to be quarried below the earth, and so buildings made of stone tend to stand out from the surrounding countryside.

But now, unwillingly, I have leave this "golden age" and come to the succeeding age of silver, in which money is used for exchange and comes to be regarded as an object of desire. Now, from the eleventh century onwards, a new civilization appears in the West, in France and England and Germany, as well as in Italy. It is associated with institutions and laws of various kinds, with the emancipation of serfs and the growth of cities, with the rise of schools and universities in place of the old monasteries, with the building of castles and churches and imposing cathedrals all in stone. And it is also associated with free movement of various kinds, movement of traders and merchants, of knights and pilgrims, of monks (no longer so severely restricted to their monasteries) and the new friars. Such a diversity of people as we find recorded towards the end of the fourteenth century in Chaucer's *Canterbury Tales*. But again I am running ahead of my story.

Here I come to yet another contrast between the city and the countryside. With the rise of the city, we come across ever new and splendid styles of architecture, first the Roman and Romanesque, and then the Gothic with its own development from early to late, from decorated to perpendicular. Of these two main styles of architecture, the Roman looks back (as its name implies) to the great city of Rome with its use of the rounded arch; but as it develops into the Romanesque from the age of Charlemagne onwards, it takes on something of the simplicity as well as the primitiveness of that "golden age". There is a real charm of childhood in almost all that survives in stone from this period. But with the urbanization and increasing sophistication of the West, the simpler Romanesque changes into the more complicated Gothic, with its intricate balancing of weights and forces, such as one finds in most of the great cathedrals of France and England, as well as those (in particular) of Cologne in West Germany and Milan in North Italy. Yet even though these new cathedrals are erected in cities, not without pomp and pride, they are much closer than the old architecture of Greece and Rome to the countryside and the forest. They may be built of stone, but their soaring structure with pointed arches, buttresses and pinnacles, is strikingly reminiscent of glades of trees in the forests of the North. In such churches the very stones seem to come alive, as above all in the great cathedral of Chartres.

It is in this context I have to introduce another great Christian saint, corresponding to St. Benedict, the father of Western monasticism. For what St. Benedict was to the monks, St. Francis of Assisi was to the friars. As the monks fitted in, with their vow of stability, to the old feudal age, when people remained in one native place from generation to generation; so the friars appropriately appear in this new age of movement, going from one town or villageto another, and preaching the Gospel wherever they go, according to the example of Jesus in his public life in Galilee. But how, we may ask, did it all begin? What was the ideal that inspired St. Francis to initiate this new movement?

From one point of view, it began with a word in the Bible, the word of Jesus to the rich young man, to whom he said (as we have seen), "If you wish to be perfect, go and sell all you have, then come and follow me." Of course, Francis had known these words from childhood, but on rereading them at a certain point in his youth he was deeply impressed by them, and he felt them as personally addressed by Jesus to himself (for he was then also a rich young man). He took the words so literally that, on meeting a beggar in Rome, he changed clothes with that beggar in order to experience the other's poverty. And what he experienced was an exhilaration of freedom: he was freed from his old life of worldly pursuits, he was free to enjoy (as he had never before enjoyed) the flowers of the field, the birds of the air, and above all the loving providence of his heavenly Father. For him these three things went inextricably together: poverty, freedom and providence; and with them went a simple, natural, primitive life as in the "golden age". All for him was new, as in a baptism of the spirit. And it was now his mission to communicate his newness to the Church of Christ.

For now, after twelve centuries, the Church of Christ had grown old, in spite of its successive movements of renewal, with the hermits of the East and the monks of the West. In a dream Francis saw a church tottering in ruin and he was told to rebuild it. At first, he took this command very literally; and on finding a local church, that of St. Damian, in disrepair, he set about repairing it. But it wasn't just a particular little church he was destined to repair; but the universal Church of Christ, as it had grown old in the world, not least in Rome. So it was to Rome that Francis with his followers made his way, in order to win the Pope's approval for his new way of life. The Pope of that time was the great Innocent III, and he was great enough to recognize the divine call of this little man from Assisi. For he, too, had a dream of a church tottering into ruin, only its wall was supported by one little man; and when Francis appeared before him, he recognized the man he had seen in his dream. And so he gave his approval and papal blessing to Francis and his followers, with their new rule of life, so different from that of St.Benedict, yet so deeply similar.

To speak in metaphorical terms, St. Benedict may have brought his monks from tle desert of Judea to the countryside of Galilee, but it was St. Francis who encouraged his friars to wander freely along the highways and byways of Galilee, preaching the gospel to the people as Jesus had done with his disciples. In that freedom there was, of course, a certain danger of exposure to the spirit of worldliness, or what St. John calls "the lust of the flesh, and the lust of the eyes and the pride of life"; and there were not a few friars who fell into this danger, as we may see in Chaucer's Friar. But for St. Francis „cl, freedom had to be based on the Christian ideal of "holy poverty", accepted not just in a spirit of ascetic duty or stern discipline, but in a spirit of love and devotion. He even personified this ideal in terms of contemporary chivalry and minstrelsy as "the Lady Poverty". For him she was a beautiful lady, commanding his undying devotion no less than other ladies were gallantly served by knights or sung by minstrels. She raised his eyes, no less surely than the Lady Philosophy had raised the eyes of the early Christian philosopher Boethius (in his book on *The Comfort of Philosophy*), from the concerns of this world to those of God in heaven.

For him, however, this "Lady Poverty" was no Platonic ideal, closing his eyes to things on earth in order to concentrate his mind on things of heaven. She rather enabled him to see things on earth, plants and animals, the sun, the moon and the stars, in a fresh light, as in the morning of the world, "when the morning stars sang together, and all the sons of God shouted for joy." So we see St. Francis, more than any other saint after him, though like many of the desert saints before him, on intimate terms with trees and flowers, and especially with birds and animals. In this respect, he became a legend in his own lifetime; and so it wasn't long after he died that this legend was set down by friars who still remembered him in the charming account known as *Fioretti*, or "'Little Flowers of St. Francis'". One such story is that of his preaching to the birds, when there were no men to listen to him – just as his follower, St. Anthony of Padua, on another occasion preached to the fishes. Another story shows him speaking sharply to a wolf that was terrorizing the people of Gubbio in much the same way as the Celtic St. Columba had preached in the seventh century to an ancestor of the Loch Ness monster. And then, of course, there is his *Canticle of the Sun* with its famous words, "Be praised, my Lord, with all your creatures, above all, Brother Sun!"

For him, in fact, not only men and women, but all creatures in heaven and on earth were his brothers and sisters, under one Father in heaven and Mary as mother. This was because Christ himself, as we read in the letter to the Hebrews, was not ashamed to call us brothers (and sisters), and because he made himself in all things like us his brothers (and sisters). This, too, is the significance of the word "friar", by which the followers of St. Francis came to be known, in contrast to the monks of St. Benedict. For "friar" is from the Latin word for "brother", *frater*. Of course, the earlier monks had addressed each other as "brother"; and in the early Church, as we read in the *Acts of the Apostles*, Christians had generally called each other "brother". Yet somehow owing to St. Francis' universal insistence on this form of address, the name has come to be specially associated with him and his followers, as well as other similar religious orders that arose in his time, such as the Dominicans or "blackfriars", the Carmelites or "white friars", while the followers of St. Francis, or Franciscans, were known as "greyfriars" (from the different colours of their habits). Thus with a word St. Francis cut through the proliferating legal forms of institutions in church and state, by laying emphasis on the Church as the family of Christ, and by seeing all men and all creatures as belonging to the same family.

6. The Cloud of Unknowing

The more I reflect on past ages, the deeper grows my conviction that historians are liars. They make such an emphatic profession of truth. They go all out for what they call historical, verifiable fact. But, I ask, is such historical, verifiable fact the same as significant fact? The facts that are recorded in historical documents are usually those that concern "very important persons" or very important events; but are these facts really so significant? It seems to me that there are two levels, or rather three, in all the ages of human history; but the attention of historians is largely taken up with the first, most superficial level, that which appears openly on the public stage in the eyes of all men. But they forget that what appears openly on the surface isn't necessarily what is most important in reality. What is most important in history, as in human life, is what is most likely to be hidden.

Take, for instance, the history of Europe in the fourteenth century, which is commonly seen as "the decline and fall" or (in the words of the Dutch scholar, Johan Huizinga) "the waning" of the Middle Ages. What do historians see as the central events of this period? Among the many recorded events of the century, pride of place must surely go to the Hundred Years War between England and France that occupied most of the period; and then, in the course of this war, there took place the disastrous calamity of the Black Death right in mid-century. But now compare these events as described by modern historians, on the basis of contemporary documents, with an equally contemporary document of a more literary nature. I mean Chaucer's *Canterbury Tales*. Here is a picture of ordinary life in England in the late fourteenth century, showing a representative cross-section of English people, both pious and not so pious, making their way as pilgrims to the shrine of St. Thomas at Canterbury. To judge from what historians say about the period, these pilgrims should be oppressed as

47

well by their recent memory of the plague that had so devastated Europe as by their awareness of the present war in France. Yet strangely enough, there is no such feeling of oppression in their minds. They seem to have forgotten all about the plague, which had not only broken out some thirty or forty years ago (that is, a whole generation ago) but had also recurred at intervals thereafter. Nor are they particularly aware of any war occurring in France. In their minds all is at peace as they travel to Canterbury, telling tales on the way; and the only breach of peace takes the form of disputes such as those between the Friar and the Summoner, or between the Host and the Pardoner. Readers of these *Tales* hardly feel they are set in the mediaeval past; there is something so strangely modern about them. But they shouldn't say "modern": they should say "human". And it belongs to a genius like Chaucer to bring out the humanity of an age, whereas historians only insist on its antiquity.

But now I wish, to turn to another level of the same age, one that is even deeper than that of the *Canterbury Tales*. Historians may take the superficial level of "very important persons" and very important events, as such appear on the public stage; while poets like Chaucer may vividly depict the lives and thoughts of very ordinary people, such as the pilgrims going to Canterbury. But now I wish to turn to the deeper currents of life and thought that affect the lives and thoughts as well of ordinary people as of "very important persons". Such are the currents that come out of the rise of the universities and the development of scholastic thought in the thirteenth century, as well as the movement of the friars I have already mentioned in connection with St. Francis of Assisi. It is a kind of paradox that St. Francis, who laid such emphasis on poverty and simplicity and a return to nature, should have sent his friars into the universities and the cities where they took their part in the growing sophistication of the age. Both in the thirteenth and in the fourteenth century, prominent among the leading scholastic thinkers are representatives of the two great orders of friars, Franciscan and Dominican. Among the Franciscans are St. Bonaventure, Duns Scotus and William of Ockham, in whom we follow a strange movement from pious devotion to arid Aristotelian logic. Among the Dominicans are St. Albert and St.Thomas Aquinas, who were the leading advocates of Aristotle in the new age, while developing a way from scholastic logic to mysticism.

I mention these thinkers not because I wish to propose a general interpretation of their thought, which can only be superficial, but because I wish to lead up to a climax in the thought of the greatest among them, St.Thomas Aquinas. He is, of course, famous for his *Summa Theologica*, or sum of all Christian theology, which may be seen as standing to his thought as *The Canterbury Tales* to the poetry of Chaucer. Now this great work of his, like Chaucer's *Canterbury Tales,* was left unfinished at his death. Why? Didn't he have the time or the energy to complete it? He had the time, but he suddenly lost the energy and the inclination, as the result of a vision he received of divine truth. In that vision it seemed to him that, by contrast, everything he had written of God and man and the world was of no more worth than a straw. And as for myself, much as I admire his *Summa,* which I have studied for some seven years in connection with my preparation for the priesthood, I admire even more deeply this culminating vision of his. For in this vision, it seems to me, he passes from the silver of words to the gold of silence.

It isn't, therefore, surprising to find that St. Thomas, for all his intellectualism, or perhaps because of it, stands at the head of a new movement of Western mysticism. In his teaching about God, he expresses a kind of religious agnosticism,when he says that we can know of God rather what he is not than what he is. In his commentaries on basic Christian texts, he specially takes up the great mystical author of the early sixth century, known as Dionysius the

Areopagite. Lastly, among his Dominican pupils not the least is the German mystical thinker known as Meister (German for Master) Eckhart; and Eckhart stands at the beginning of an important line of German and Dutch thinkers who appear on the banks of the river Rhine during the fourteenth century. But again, I only mention them in order to lead up to a certain anonymous English mystic, who appears towards the end of this period about the same time as Chaucer was writing his *Canterbury Tales*. I mean the author of the mystical treatise, *The Cloud of Unknowing*. Though we know nothing about him, who he was or where he lived, at least his writings show that he came under the influence of St.Thomas and the Dominicans from Eckhart onwards. It was also he who translated the treatise of Dionysius the Areopagite on mystical theology, under the English title of *Hid Divinity* (where "divinity" is the old English word for "theology", while "hid" is his rendering of "mystical").

If I mention this author here and give him pride of place in this discussion of the fourteenth century, it isn't because I have found him emphasized in histories of mediaeval thought, though he sometimes is emphasized, but because in my own reading of various mediaeval writers I have found his words most readable, most refreshing and most deeply impressive. Other authors may be more famous, partly for their more voluminous works, partly for their wider, more clearly recognizable influence on their contemporaries; whereas this author seems to be as hid as his divinity and his own identity. Yet I have to confess I have come across few Christian authors – and I have read many – who are so simple, yet so profound, and so charming in style and sentence, as this English author.

Well, what is so charming about this author? First, there is his charming invitation tothe reader of his book (which existed only in manuscript and wasn't printed until the end of the seventeenth century), "What weary, wretched heart, and sleeping in sloth, is that which is not wakened with the drawing of this love and the voice of this calling?" It is an invitation which appealed to the heart of no less a modern poet than T.S.Eliot, and which he incorporates at the climax of his own mystical poem, "Little Gidding", which is the last of his *Four Quartets*. Following this invitation, we find that we are paradoxically called to nothing less than nothing! – or rather, nothing but God, which is prcisely the meaning of that "holy poverty" taught and practised by St. Francis of Assisi. "Lift up your heart to God," says the author, "with a meek stirring of love, and seek him and none of his goods. And further, make sure you seek nothing but him, so that nothing may work in your mind or your will but only him." As for all matters, he continues, "Do what you can to forget all the creatures that God ever made and the works of them, so that neither your thought nor your desire may be directed or extended to any of them, neither in general nor in special. But let them be, and pay no heed to them." This is what he means by "the cloud of unknowing" that has to come down between a man and the world around him, or (as he also calls it) a "cloud of forgetting", while in the man there remains only "a naked intent to God".

Such is his simple teaching, as he derives it from Dionysius the Areopagite, by way of St.Thomas Aquinas and Meister Eckhart. It is such an easy teaching, in contrast to the complications of Western society and Western thought – which I deliberately call Western rather than Christian. In the society and thought of the West, especially in the period of what is called the Middle Ages (so mistakenly lumped by common readers with what they call the "dark ages"), there is so much complication and sophistication, with greed and corruption, that the Christian sources of life and culture are soon lost from sight. It is only in such "timeless moments" of perception, such as the ideal of St.Francis and the vision of St.Thomas and the "naked intent" of this anonymous author, that one perceives the true significance of Western history and culture. For, as T.S.Eliot again comments in his "Little Gidding", as a prelude to the above-mentioned quotation from *The Cloud*, "History is a pattern of timeless moments."

In such works of mediaeval mysticism, I notice two interesting points, in relation to contemporary Japan. One is a strange parallel between this insistence on "nothing" and a "cloud of forgetting" in *The Cloud* and the Buddhist ideal of *mu* at the heart of Zen meditation. Here is West and there is East, here is Christianity and there is Buddhism; and never, we think (as in the opening words of an oft-quoted poem by Kipling), "the twain shall meet". Yet the teaching is so strangely similar, as based on the mind and heart of man; and man is always and everywhere basically the same. The other point is a strong contrast, as a deep reaction, between this simple, almost wordless mysticism (for that is the literal meaning of "mysticism", to keep one's mouth shut and to say only "mmm") and the endless logical subtleties of contemporary scholasticism. It was, interestingly, against this latter logic-chopping that the later humanists, such as Erasmus and Moore, raised their voices of protest; and yet it was this same logic-chopping, as practised at the mediaeval universities, that fostered the rise of the new scientific mentality culminating in the genius of Galileo.

But if the author of *The Cloud* is so anonymous, and if his writings remained in only a few manuscripts till the end of the seventeenth century, what can we say of his influence or that of his fellow mystics on his age, soon to be the age of the Renaissance? Well, I think I can find traces of his, or at least their, influence in three important works of the fifteenth and the sixteenth century, whose authors are more or less known to us. First, there is the great Christian classic, *The Imitation of Christ*, commonly attributed to the Dutchman, Thomas A Kempis, though assigned by some to the great scholar of the University of Paris, John Gerson. Here, too, we find a strong reaction against the definitions and distinctions of contemporary scholasticism, as in the famous saying, "I would rather feel compunction than know its definition." This book also comes close to *The Cloud* in its teaching, which also echoes that of St. Francis on holy poverty, "Give all for all, and you will find all." Needless to say, the common source of this teaching is to be found in the gospel of Jesus Christ. I might add, concerning the influence of this book, that, though it seems a pious treatise for a few devout Christians, it was, after the Bible, the biggest best-seller not just of its own time but for ages to come – as may be seen from its numerous translations (from the original Latin) and from its almost innumerable editions and impressions once the age of printing had set in. Indeed, the bibliographical history of *The Imitation* stands in sharp contrast to that of *The Cloud*.

Secondly, there is an interesting continuation of the English mysticism of *The Cloud*, with its insistence on "nothing" or an emptying of the self, and the better known Spanish mysticism of *The Dark Night of the Soul*, whose author is clearly identified as St. John of the Cross, who helped to found the reformed order of Carmelite friars. In St. John we generally see the climax of the Christian mystical tradition, both in his poems and in his various prose commentaries on his poems. He is also seen as taking a prominent place in Renaissance Spanish literature, as a poet and prose author; but more than his style of words is the deep, insistent message in his thoughts, or rather his spiritual experiences. Whether he knew *The Cloud* or not, there is a marked similarity between that "cloud" of mysticism and his "dark night", a similarity that consists in the experience of *mu* or "nothing". And yet, out of that "nothing, comes everything, or to put it in Shakespeare's words, "Nothing brings me all things." Another interesting point in common between *The Cloud* and *The Dark Night* is the way they both come together in the mystical poetry of T.S.Eliot's *Four Quartets*. Here, in the poem "East Coker", the reader is mystified by a series of paradoxical negatives, which sound almost like Zen *kōan*: "In order to arrive at what you do not know you must go by a way which is the way of ignorance. In order to possess what you do not possess, you must go by the way of dispossession. In order to arrive at what you are not, you must go through the way in which you are not. And what you do not know is the only thing you know; and what you own is what you do not own; and where you are is where you are not."

Thirdly, and above all, there is a direct line of influence, if not from *The Cloud*, at least from *The Imitation of Christ* on *The Spiritual Exercises* of St. Ignatius. Only, here we have no confrontation with, or reaction against, scholastic philosophy, but a simple ignoring of the whole Western tradition of philosophy and theology in favour of the Gospel of Jesus Christ. Not that St. Ignatius intends a rejection of that tradition, like Martin Luther; but while receiving it, he makes no explicit use of it but prefers to concentrate on its divine source. For this purpose we may follow what he himself saw as a spiritual pilgrimage, from the stage of a hermit to that of a pilgrim, and from the stage of a friar to that of founder of a new religious order of priests, the Society of Jesus. It is only from the time of this foundation, in 1540, that St. Ignatius emerges into the public view of history as one of the "very important persons" of the sixteenth century. For the Society he founded was to prove one of the most important influences on what is called the "counter-Reformation" movement in Catholic Europe, both for its educational and for its missionary activities. But, as usual, historians get everything wrong in their concern for outward appearances and their neglect of the inner reality. In this case, the outward appearances are the activities of the Jesuit order under the wise direction of St. Ignatius; but the inner reality is the book of *Exercises*, which he composed while still a hermit in the lonely cave of Manresa in the North-East of Spain. Here he looks back, with the desert fathers of Egypt, to the example of Jesus' fasting and prayer in the desert, and also with St. Francis, to the ideal of holy poverty and preaching shown by Jesus in his public life. He also leads up, like the author of *The Cloud*, to "the drawing of this love and the voice of this calling" in what he calls the "election". Then the one making the "exercises" is encouraged not only to listen to the voice of divine love but also to respond with the entire gift and surrender of himself, giving all (as A Kempis puts it) to receive all. And there he touches on the heart not just of Western but rather of universal Christian culture.

7. Under the Greenwood Tree

"After the darkness of the Dark Ages and the waning of the Middle Ages comes a miraculous rebirth and renewal, the Renaissance! An age of new life, new vigour, new ideas, new discoveries, new inventions! Christopher Columbus discovers a New World, and Vasco da Gama discovers a new sea route to the old world of Asia! An age of artistic genius in Italy, with Leonardo Da Vinci and Michelangelo! An age of new learning in the North, with Erasmus and Thomas More! An age of religious reformation in Germany and Switzerland, with Luther and Calvin! An age of new science in Germany and Italy, with Copernicus and Galileo! An age of new riches pouring into Europe as never before, from the silver mines of Mexico and the gold mines of Peru and from trade with India and the Indies along the new sea-routes opened up by the Portuguese! An age of new finance and commerce, of usury and capitalism, of ambitious enterprises reaching out to the ends of the earth! An age no longer restrained by religious or moral scruple, but straining to realize the utmost possibilities of human endeavour!"

Such an enthusiastic view of the Renaissance has been all too common in the past; and even today its echoes are still to be heard in classes of world history, where the events and movements of the past are inevitably compressed into sweeping generalizations. But today we are coming to have our doubts about the validity of such a view. Especially on the occasion of the fifth centenary of Columbus' so-called "discovery" of the New World, so far from making it an object of celebration, people – not least in America – have presented it as an object of lamentation. So far from praising the new age as one of vigour and expansion, people are more disposed nowadays to criticize it as one of unparalleled greed and aggression. In the Middle Ages there were at least strict laws against usury, which applied at least to Christians; but with the undermining of Church control after the Reformation, the relaxation of these laws, especially in Protestant countries like England and Holland, led to the emergence of capitalism and modern finance. In the Middle Ages the power of the king was limited by the power not only of the Church but also of the barons; but with the Renaissance we find the emergence of nation-states with more power gathered into the hands of individual rulers, such as the great Emperor Charles V and King Henry VIII of England. Even the rise of science, which used to seem an absolute good for mankind, is now seen to have its culmination in the atomic bomb that destroyed the city of Hiroshima in 1945. And since then we seem to have been living under the shadow not just of atomic but of hydrogen bombs and other modern technological weapons of destruction. It is almost a marvel that we are still here to shake our heads over the benefits of modern science!

All this, however, is but (as I have pointed out) on the mere surface of history, whether we lavish praise on the achievements of the Renaissance or shake our heads over its long-term effects. But what is below that glittering surface? And who is to lead us to a recognition of the harsh reality? Who but the great dramatic genius of the new age, William Shakespeare? Usually, historians are more interested in the outward events of the age, as recorded in political documents which inevitably overlook as well the stage in general as the genius of Shakespeare in particular. On the other hand, literary scholars are more interested in the plays as written for and presented on the Elizabethan stage, without considering how far they mirror the age in which they were composed. Or if they do attend to Hamlet's description of players and their plays as "the abstracts and brief chronicles of the time", they mostly assume that Shakespeare was the national poet and dramatist of England's glory under the royal patronage of a queen known as Gloriana. Yet if there is any moral lesson to be found in the plays of Shakespeare, as indeed it is to be found in every play, it is a continually repeated warning

57

against trusting to outward appearances and overlooking the hidden reality. As Bassanio says in *The Merchant of Venice*, as he comes to make his choice among the three caskets of gold, silver and lead, "So may the outward shows be least themselves: the world is still deceived with ornament."

Take this well-known play, *The Merchant of Venice*, for example. So much of the discussion on it today seems to concern itself with the tragedy of Shylock the Jew and the problem of contemporary anti-Semitism. Yet the play is neither an attack on Jews nor a defence of them, though it admittedly contains elements of both attack and defence. Shakespeare is nothing if not impartial. But on a deeper level, the play reflects the commercial and financial problems of the age, that of the new usury and rise of capitalism and that of the new greed for money. In contrast to the mediaeval mentality of Christians like Antonio, Shylock stands for the increasingly lucrative practice of usury – though in the course of the play we find him preferring his lust for revenge over that for gold. Nor is it only Jews like Shylock who are swayed by this "accursed thirst for gold"; but the the two princes of Arragon and Morocco, who are respectively (I suppose) Christian and Moslem, are shown as attracted by silver and gold in their respective choice among the caskets. But, as the Prince of Morocco finds inside the casket of gold, and as Shakespeare thereby reminds his audiences, "All that glisters is not gold." This is, in fact, the consideration that prompts Bassanio a little later to make his choice of the leaden casket; and inside he discovers the picture of Portia, with commendation of those "that choose not by the view", moreover, in his choice of this casket, he comments, "Thy plainness moves me more than eloquence" – which in this context strangely evokes the ideal of the Lady Poverty as pursued by St. Francis of Assisi.

Needless to say, this isn't the only problem dealt with in the dramatic terms of the play. But as we move with

Bassanio and Portia from the plot of the three caskets to that of the pound of flesh, so we move from the contrast between appearances and reality to the further contrast between legal justice and divine mercy. If the dramatist had intended to present Shylock as a tragic victim persecuted by Christians like Antonio, he surely chose a strange way of doing so. For in the trial scene that is the famous climax of this play, it is rather Shylock who is shown as persecutor and Antonio as victim; and while Shylock insists on his narrow conception of legal justice, which is but a disguise for unreasoning revenge, Portia appeals to the heavenly ideal of mercy. It may be a mere legal quibble that enables Portia to triumph over Shylock, as not a few modern commentators point out; but in the mind of Shakespeare and the clear context of the play, it is rather heaven that triumphs over earth, and divine mercy over human or rather legal justice. And it is on the note of the heavenly music of the spheres that the play draws to its happy ending, as Lorenzo tells his newly baptized love Jessica: "How sweet the moonlight sleeps upon this bank! Here will we sit, and let the sounds of music creep in our ears. Soft stillness and the night become the touches of sweet harmony."

No less impressive for its insistence on the reality lurking beneath the false appearances of the world is the subsequent comedy of *As You Like It*. So far from being deceived, like the majority of Elizabethan historians, by the glitter of Elizabeth's court, Shakespeare seems to have nothing but scorn to cast on what he calls in this play the "painted pomp" and "peril" of "the envious court". Here precisely is a play composed according to his heart, as its very title seems to imply. Its whole movement is from the court and city in the first Act, where there is nothing but envy and distrust and fraternal rivalry, recalling the original rivalry of Cain against Abel, to the Forest of Arden from the second Act onwards. Its ideal is the old pastoral ideal of "the golden world", where "a many merry men" live with the exiled Duke "like the old Robin Hood of England"; and here they "fleet the time carelessly", dining on venison and singing sweet songs (according to the title of one) "under the greenwood tree". Yet the reality is one of exile, for these men from the Duke downwards are all outlaws under the new laws of the usurping Duke; and in the forest they have to endure "the penalty of Adam, the seasons' difference", such as "the icy fang and churlish chiding of the winter's wind". On the other hand, once they grow accustomed to this reality, they find it full of unsuspected sweetness. As the Duke declares, with all but explicit echoes of *The Imitation of Christ*, "Sweet are the uses of adversity"; and he continues, in words that reverberate in the ears of generations of English schoolboys, "And this our life, exempt from public haunt, finds tongues in trees, books in the running brooks, sermons in stones, and good in every thing."

Indeed, we may well feel, this Duke is all but in name a follower of St. Francis of Assisi. And what is more, these words of his strangely echo those of the Franciscan Friar Laurence in *Romeo and Juliet*, where the latter exclaims – also in his opening speech, and also with an echo of another passage in *The Imitation* – "Nought so vile that on the earth doth live, but to the earth some special good doth give." Both speeches, that of the Duke and that of the Friar, give utterance to Shakespeare's own love, as a countryman, of the English countryside, a love of all plants and animals with a minute knowledge of their names and properties. Nor is Friar Laurence the only friar to be presented, favourably, in Shakespeare's plays, as the trusted adviser of hero and heroine. Also in the comedy of *Much Ado About Nothing*, we see the figure of Friar Francis offering wise advice to the poor heroine, whose name is Hero. And then, in the later "problem" comedy of *Measure for Measure*, we see the more complex figure of a duke turned friar, as Friar Lodowick, giving advice to both the unfortunate lovers, Claudio and Juliet. Moreover, what is common to the advice of all three friars (though in the first case, the advice is frustrated of its purpose) is a movement from the outward appearance of death to the reality of life, as when Friar Francis tells Hero, "Come, lady, die to live."

Now to return to the original theme of the contrast between reality and appearances, there is no play in which it is more strongly emphasized than in *Hamlet*; and perhaps for this reason, it marks a notable turning-point in Shakespeare's dramatic career, between his happy comedies and his great tragedies, as also between the Elizabethan and the Jacobean age and between the sixteenth and the seventeenth century. And in this play, this contrast between reality and appearances is set in a dramatic situation which only seems to be mediaeval and Danish but is, in fact, awkwardly close to Elizabethan England. For one thing, it gives the lie to those who like to regard Shakespeare as the poetic spokesman for his queen and country, the patriotic singer of England's greatness. The setting of the court is splendid, but it is no less charged with envy and peril than the new court of *As You Like It*; and in such a setting Hamlet, no less than Rosalind in the other play, feels himself out of place, if not in a metaphorical prison. He can only express his deepest thoughts in soliloquy; but in company he has to hold his tongue and eventually die of a broken heart. "To be, or not to be: that is the question" not only of Hamlet in mediaeval Denmark, under the new regime of Claudio, but also of Shakespeare in Elizabethan England, as he gives similar utterance to it in his own person in the Sonnet beginning with the words, "Tired with all these, for restful death I cry...."

And so I pass from *Hamlet*, as the first, to *King Lear* as (in my opinion) the last and greatest of the four "great tragedies" of Shakespeare. Here, too, we find in a more deeply tragic form the situation of *As You Like It*, in which the good characters are all, one by one, driven from court or city to the countryside or forest or wilderness. As we follow Lear, in particular, into this wilderness, on the heath in the storm, we hardly feel (like the Duke in *As You Like It*) the sweetness of adversity, but we are impressed rather by the bitterness of his indignation against his two daughters for their unnatural ingratitude. Yet it is in the storm that he gradually comes to a knowledge of himself, if only when he confronts the form of a mad beggar, Edgar, and exclaims, "Thou art the thing itself!" Before, he had indignantly demanded, "Who is it that can tell me who I am?" And now, it is as if Edgar, rather than the Fool, gives him the answer, "I can", and even "I am." But it is also out of the storm, that he comes to confront not only the pitiful Edgar, but also his pitying daughter Cordelia. And it is in this culminating scene of reunion between the mad old father and his loving daughter, that, even more feelingly than in *As You Like It*, we are shown "the uses of adversity." For, as Kent has previously commented, "Nothing almost sees miracles but misery." And now in, or out of, his misery, Lear sees the miracle of his good daughter coming to him and forgiving him and raising him up, like the good father in Christ's parable of the prodigal son. So when Lear recognizes "this lady to be my child Cordelia", she simply answers, with an echo (which is, I am sure, deliberately intended by the dramatist) of the divine name, "And so I am, I am!"

What is more, all this immense happiness, a happiness that is not of this world but belongs to the other world beyond the grave, comes (as Shakespeare shows) literally out of "nothing". Indeed, I am convinced there is nothing so deep, in all his plays as this all but metaphysical contrast between being and non-being, between everything and nothing. It is at least implicit in all the plays; but to speak only of *King Lear*, it is significant how the two plots, centring respectively on the old king and his nobleman the Earl of Gloucester, begin with a quibbling exchange on "Nothing". When asked by her father what she can say "to draw a third (part of the kingdom) more opulent than your sisters", Cordelia can only answer "Nothing" – as in truth there is no other answer to such a question. But Lear, misunderstanding her true meaning, replies, "Nothing will come of nothing" – precisely echoing an axiom in Aristotelian philosophy, assuming a merely empty nothing; whereas Cordelia's is a full, creative nothing, the utterance of her true love. Similarly, in the other plot, to Gloucester's question, "What paper were you reading?" Edmund falsely replies, "Nothing, my lord." Then his father insists, "The quality of nothing hath not such need to hide itself. Let's see; come. If it be nothing. I shall not need spectacles." Thus both old men are deceived, in different ways, by "nothing"; and so they both, in their different ways, come to "nothing", at first in madness and blindness, and eventually in death. Yet they both come, paradoxically through their respective experiences of "nothing" to the deeper experience of everything, as Lear is reunited with his dear daughter Cordelia, and Gloucester is reunited with his loyal son Edgar. Then if they die, as they both do most piteously, it is not merely in an excess of sorrow, but rather in a strange conflict "twixt two extremes of passion, joy and grief"; and if their hearts burst, they do so "smilingly."

And this, we may conclude is Shakespeare's implicit comment not just on the imagined fate of Lear and Gloucester in prehistoric Britain, some seven centuries before Christ, but on the situation of his own "poor country" (as he also calls it in *Macbeth*) and on himself as well. It isn't mere tragedy, still less (as some modern critics imagine) absurdity, but a poverty and a persecution out of which good is drawn in the kind plan of divine providence. As Hamlet comes to realize in the last Act of his play, "And that should teach us, there's a divinity that shapes our ends, rough-hew them how we will." And as St. Paul assures the faithful at Rome, "All things work together for good, to those who love God."

8. The Noble Savage

When Christopher Columbus first set foot on American soil, he did more than merely discover a new world in the West – from the viewpoint of the old world in Europe. He was also initiating the modern world. At least, one may well maintain that October 12, 1492, saw the end of the Middle Ages and the beginning of a new, modern age. At least, his discovery for Spain and the whole of Europe led the way to further discoveries, till the globe was first circumnavigated by Magellan or rather (as he died on the way, in the Philippines) by his sailors in 1519-21. And so for the first time since man spread out over the earth from the mythical Garden of Eden, the world was one. For the first time. Westerners came to the Far East of Asia, as well as to the Far West of America, and so the extremes of the earth were joined together. Thus it was in the context of such a vast widening of horizons in all directions that, we may say, modern man was born.

But, we may ask, was this such a good thing – whether for the discoverers or for the discovered? For Spain, a whole new world was opened up not only for exploration, but also for exploitation – especially when silver mines were found in Mexico, and gold mines in Peru. The Westerners had come as conquerors, or in Spanish *conquistadores,* and they considered it their right of conquest to pillage the new-found lands of their almost limitless supplies of gold and silver, and to send them back home to Spain. Not all of it, however, went to Spain; but on the way, some of the ships were wrecked and their treasure lost at the bottom of the sea, while other ships were taken by pirates, especially English pirates, and brought to other countries, especially England. Anyhow, the lands of the old world were soon flooded with all this gold and silver, and the accompanying "accursed thirst for gold" and silver. Culturally, it came to seem as if the new age, with so many new opportunities for artists and such rich material for their artistic skill, was literally a golden age. Yet, as we have seen, a true "golden age" is an age rather of poverty and simple innocence than of such untold wealth. And morally, as such money always does, it ushered in a new age of cruelty and corruption.

Yet the discovery did indeed awaken the old dream of a "golden age", in the examples of innocence that were now revealed by discoverers of the West from Columbus onwards. Wherever Western sailors landed along the East coast of America, they came across primitive people, whom they mistakenly called "Indians" (without realizing there lay an even wider ocean than the Atlantic between them and India); and the innocent lives and gentle behaviour of these people they often described in glowing terms to their friends back home. It even seemed to some of them that they had found not just a new world but a Garden of Eden, peopled by innocent men and women like Adam and Eve before the Fall. Only, when they came across further evidence of warfare among the different tribes of these people, and then, worse than warfare, evidence of cannibalism practised on the defeated tribes, not just spasmodically out of a primitive passion, but systematically in the highly sophisticated Aztec culture of Mexico, did they have second thoughts. And then the primitive man came to be seen as "savage".

Still, for the time being, the discovery of new men in the New World awoke all kinds of dreams and visions among writers in the old world. First, we have the famous *Utopia* of the great English humanist, Sir Thomas More; though his invented land is by no means primitive but as civilized as the lands of the Aztecs and the Incas, or even more so. Nor is it merely an ideal republic, like the old ideal of Plato, but rather a convenient means for the author to satirize the real conditions of life back in England. The same may be said of the French humanist Montaigne's essay "Of the Cannibals", which is more directly inspired by the accounts of primitive men found on the shores of America. He echoes the glowing terms of these accounts, even while admitting that these simple, innocent people have the unfortunate habit of eating each other when they go to war; but his real purpose is not so much to praise them, whom he has never met, as to criticize his contemporaries, against whom he has many grudges. Thirdly, both More's *Utopia* and Montaigne's essay may be seen as influences on Shakespeare's last play, *The Tempest*, in which the good old man Gonzalo describes an imaginary commonwealth, echoing the very words of Montaigne but in the spirit of More's "merry fooling".

Incidentally, the term "the New World" is first found in the English language as the title of a book published in 1555 by a man appropriately named Richard Eden, *The Decades of the New World or West India*. And it was in an enlarged version of this book, published in 1577, that English readers were first informed of the existence and nature of Japan from the eye-witness accounts of Jesuit missionaries. But it is in Shakespeare's *Tempest* that the term received a wider currency, in the innocent exclamation of the heroine Miranda on seeing so many fine noblemen in the simple cave of her father Prospero, "O, wonder! How many goodly creatures are there here! How beauteous mankind is! O brave new world, that has such people in't!" Of course, she is speaking not of primitive people in America but of sophisticated European noblemen, whom she sees for the first time. It is as if the simple natives had given utterance to such words on first seeing Columbus and his followers. Nor is the play set in America at all, but on a lonely island in the Mediterranean on which the above-mentioned noblemen have been wrecked by the magic art of Prospero. Still, it may be said that America is evidently in the mind and intention of the dramatist, as the inspiration for this his last play came from contemporary accounts of a shipwreck suffered by a ship of the Virginia fleet on the Bermudas in the year 1609. Only, the dramatist for reasons of his own transposes the coast of the Bermudas to an island in the Mediterranean between

Tunis and Naples.

In the literature that has been provoked by the recent celebrations, and denunciations, of the fifth centenary of Columbus' arrival on the coast of America, not a few literary critics have come up with a new interpretation of *The Tempest*. In their eyes, the magician Prospero is typical of the new colonizers and exploiters of the New World, especially in relation to the first native of the island, named Caliban (a name no doubt derived from the similar "cannibal"). Certainly, in some ways, Prospero seems all too domineering as well towards Miranda's new found lover, Prince Ferdinand, as towards his slave Caliban. He justifies his attitude on the grounds that, after having been well treated at first, Caliban had tried to rape his daughter Miranda; and so Caliban's slavery is only a just punishment. But the punishment does nothing to improve Caliban's character; and when he gets the chance, on his meeting with two drunken sailors from the shipwreck, he seeks revenge against his master. No doubt, in the dramatist's intention, Prospero is the hero of this play, while Caliban is a kind of villain, if only in the comic sub-plot. Yet the portrayal of Caliban is by no means unkind; but if he is lustful and vengeful, on the one hand, he is also shown as a lover of nature on his island home, on the other. So many modern Americans find it easier to sympathize with Caliban as their fellow-countryman or even ancestor, than with the European Prospero – though it was no fault of poor Prospero that he originally came to this lonely island, banished as he was by his wicked brother Antonio.

Anyhow, here we have two kinds of American native projected on the minds, and the consciences, of men in Europe, one noble and the other savage. And together they give rise, as never before, to new discussions among theologians and philosophers on "the state of nature". Previously, the old discussions had revolved round the mythical state of Adam, both before and after the Fall, both in the Garden of Eden and in the wilderness of the outside world. But now European theologians and philosophers come to consider this state as a present reality, if beyond the ocean. And, as is inevitable with European individualism, different men come up with different opinions on this subject. On the one hand, the "savage" view may be represented by Thomas Hobbes, who in his famous *Leviathan* considers the life of man in the state of nature (which is for him a state of war) to be "solitary, poor, nasty, brutish and short". It is a definitely pessimistic view, the idea that men are born evil and this evil in them has to be eradicated by education and severe discipline. On the other hand, the "noble" view may be represented by Hobbes' successor, John Locke, who in his no less famous essay on *Civil Government* describes the state of nature, if somewhat abstractly, as "a state of perfect freedom" and "a state of equality". His, view may thus be compared to the idea that all meen are naturally good and this good in them has but to be fostered or drawn out by kindly education. It was, however, the contemporary poet, John Dryden, who gave chief currency to the idea of "the noble savage", in his character of Almanzor in *The Conquest of Granada*. Here the hero boldly declares: "I am as free as nature first made man, ere the base laws of servitude began, when wild in woods the noble savage ran."

Almost two centuries divide Christopher Columbus, who first encountered the "noble savage" in America, from John Dryden, who gave chief currency to the idea with his skill in words. In between the death of the one (1506) and the birth of the other (1631), there took place the religious reformation initiated by Martin Luther in 1517 and the rise of science associated with the names of Copernicus and Galileo. And both the reformation and the new science also came to centre on the idea of "nature", though from rather different points of view.

To begin with Luther, we may think of him as the bold champion of individual liberty and conscience against the orthodox tradition of the Church; and so he was, to some extent. Yet at the same time, in his new teaching he insisted on the corruption of human nature as a result of the original sin of Adam. For him man was no longer free to work out his own salvation, but a slave to sin; and it was only by means of faith, as a free gift of God, that man could rise above the darkness of his reason and the sinfulness of his nature. And so in his famous controversy with the humanist Erasmus, while he emphasized the slavery of man's will, the other took his stand on the freedom of that will. Thus we may see as it were a direct line from the pessimism of Luther to that of Hobbes. And in between them, we may recognize the accents of Luther in the words of Hamlet, who (it may be remembered) has had his education at Luther's Wittenburg, "What should such fellows as I do, crawling between earth and heaven? We are arrant knaves, all; believe none of us,"

Yet when we turn from the already old reformation to the new science of Galileo, we feel a change as it were from a Northern winter to a Mediterranean spring. In England, the great herald of the new science is a follower of Luther and a contemporary of Shakespeare, Sir Francis Bacon. In the first place, he saw himself as a great explorer, like Columbus, entrusted by God with the providential mission of inaugurating a new era of scientific discovery. And as a follower of Luther, he aimed at doing for the academic world what Luther had done for the religious world, by bringing about a reformation of learning that would expose the falsity of human tradition and begin again from the true foundations of knowledge in experience. Thus whereas Luther had returned to the Book of Scripture, to undermine the tradition of the Church, Bacon proposed to return to the other Book of Nature, with a similar purpose in mind.

Only, whereas Luther had emphasized the nature of man in his condition of sinful slavery after the Fall, and so tended to fall himself into the pessimistic view, it was Bacon's proposal to study the state of nature in iitself, as it had proceeded in the beginning from the hands of the

Creator. For him nature was good, and so was the study of nature; but many of his fellow Protestants were less optimistic, recalling as they did the divine warning to Adam and Eve against the tree of knowledge. Didn't this warning apply no less to men after the Fall than it did to Adam and Eve before the Fall? Such was their reasoning, based on the Bible. Bacon, however, rejected their fears, saying, "Let no man, upon a weak conceit of sobriety or an ill-applied moderation, think or maintain that a man can search too far, or be too well studied in the book of God's word, or in the book of God's works." Rather, he urged, "let men endeavour an endless progress or proficience in both"; and his urging has been zealously followed, if not by all who shared his religious faith, at least by all scientists from his day till today. Only, today (as I have mentioned above) we may have our doubts about Bacon's wisdom, in view of the subsequent achievements of science as well for evil as for good. Indeed, in experimental science we may all too easily recognize the allegorical tree of the knowledge of good and evil.

Moreover, it should be noted that in his approach to knowledge Bacon did not limit himself to the delighted contemplation of the world, like philosophers in former ages. For him, "knowledge in itself is power"; and it is, he remarked, by obeying nature and the laws of nature that we can command her. In a sense, he was a magician, like Shakespeare's Prospero; since by exploring the hidden secrets of nature, he expected to work all kinds of miracles – as indeed he did, if not in person, at least through those who followed his ideal of experimental science. In this respect, too, he may be compared (less favourably) with Columbus: in that, just as Columbus and his followers exploited the rich mines of the New World for the benefit of Europe, so Bacon and his followers exploited the mines of the old world, or rather of nature itself, for the benefit of man. And so he proposed a new interpretation of Genesis, where God says to Adam and Eve, "Be fruitful and multiply, and fill the earth and subdue it." Traditionally, this text was taken to mean no more than the way farmers till the earth, whether in the East or in the West, for the producing of their daily bread. But now it came to be taken as a divine permission for man to exploit the earth's resources with the same freedom as is permitted to scientific knowledge. But in view of the outcome of this interpretation today, with the rapidly increasing depletion of earth's resources, we have reason enough to doubt the wisdom of Bacon's optimism.

Finally, following in the line of reformation and rejection of Catholic tradition, we come from Luther and Bacon to the great Puritan poet, John Milton. After all, in a chapter on "the noble savage" and the state of nature, it is only natural for us to lead up to the great poet of *Paradise Lost*. It was no accident for Milton, as a Puritan, to choose this subject "of man's first disobedience and the fruit of that forbidden tree" for his long considered epic. As a humanist, he was drawn to the subject of Man, whom he presents in his glowing portrayal of Adam and Eve in Eden before the Fall in Book IV; and as a Puritan, he was drawn no less to the temptation and Fall of Man, which he naturally attributes to "the infernal serpent". Thus he looks back both, with Bacon, to the ideal state of nature and of Man, and, with Luther, to the sin of Man. If I mention him here, however, it isn't so much to introduce a discussion of his *Paradise Lost* or his ideas on man in the state of nature, as rather to indicate the connection between the rise of Puritanism and the rise of science in the seventeenth century. To some extent, there is an opposition between the two, as the Puritans were often fanatics with their insistence on "faith alone", whereas the scientists were eminently men of reason. But what they have in common is their rejection of tradition, as embodied in the Catholic Church, and their affirmation of origins whether in scripture or in nature. Moreover, they both turn away from metaphorical ornamentation and elaboration, which goes with tradition, in favour of simplicity of thought and expression. True, in

71

Milton's *Paradise Lost* we still find considerable elaboration, from the influence of his humanist education; but as we pass from his better known *Paradise Lost* to his own preferred *Paradise Regained*, we notice an increase in Puritan simplicity, if not severity. And such is the movement not only in the mind and style of Milton, but also in the age as a whole. For it is only after the Restoration of 1660, with the seeming defeat of the Puritans and the rise of the Royal Society, that we begin to breathe the air of the modern world.

9. Behold the Child!

There is something very adult, very reasonable and very restricted about the so-called "enlightenment". It is the time when what was born in the "renaissance" comes, as it were, to maturity, the period that stretches from Locke and Newton in England, to Voltaire and Rousseau in France. It is an age of secularism, when even men who are devout Christians like Dr. Johnson conceal their religious feelings in public; and so we notice towards the end of the seventeenth century an almost abrupt termination of religious subjects in art, as the "baroque" turns to the "rococo". Puritanism itself changes from a religious to moralistic movement; while scientists, who from Galileo to Newton had aimed at demonstrating the existence and wisdom of God in the visible universe, become increasingly preoccupied with the visible, tangible, measurable aspects of the material world. And always at the back of their mind is the Baconian principle that "knowledge is power", that by exploring and exploiting the hidden secrets of nature men have the power to become as gods, knowing good and evil.

This is also an age of revolution, or at least an age set between two revolutions, the first in England and the next in France. Both appear as assertions of the power of the people against the power of the king, whether James II in England or Louis XVI in France, and thus as the origins of modern democracy. At the same time, they may also be seen as revolutions against the Catholic Church; as the Catholic James II was forced out of his kingdom by the Protestant aristocracy and the Whig (or anti-Catholic) party, and the "Christian king" Louis XVI was brought to the scaffold by the anti-religious Jacobins. In between these two revolutions all seems peaceful, even dull, apart from the Seven Years War between England and France in the eighteenth century; and even that was largely fought out in the distant colonies of Canada and India. But also in between them there was taking place a different kind of revolution, first in the fields of the countryside, then in the factories of new industrial towns. It is what we call first the "agrarian" and then the "industrial" revolution. This revolution belongs to the Age of Reason, in that it appears as a "rationalizing" of economic power and a using of man-power in the most efficient, if inhuman manner. It takes place, moreover, under the auspices of the triumphant Whig party, with its almost undisputed control of government during the first half of the eighteenth century; as it was the party not only of Protestantism but also of commercialism and capitalism, not to mention colonialism.

Somehow it all fits together, with the turning away from tradition, in religion, politics, society, economics and ordinary life, everything has to be new; and that means, in this new age of "enlightenment", everything has to be rational, secular and mechanized. For now, from Newton onwards, it is an age of inventions, an age of projects and enterprises, an age of machines. With the rationalizing of agriculture in the countryside, fewer men are needed to look after the fields, and more men are crowded into the towns in search of jobs. And the jobs are awaiting them, with the newly invented machines in the factories, controlled by rational, enterprising, profit-seeking employers. And the material for the factories and their machines is being imported in increasing quantity from the colonies in America and Asia. And what is imported as material is in turn exported in the form of finished goods of all kinds. And so England becomes – as Japan has more recently become – "the factory of the world". And so, it must be added, the rich become richer and the poor become poorer, if with a relatively prosperous middle-class of "bourgeois" in between. When, however, we turn from the annals of history to those of literature, which is (in my opinion) much more reliable for understanding the hearts of the people, we find a growing chorus not of praise for England's greatness but of lament over ruin. It may be the age of the national anthem, "God Save the King", and the Union Jack, of new army regiments and "hearts of oak" in the navy, and of a patriotism that comes to its climax under Queen Victoria in the following century. But all this new patriotism seems strangely shallow and sentimental; and owing to its encouragement by the Whigs it is dismissed by the Tory Dr. Johnson as "the last refuge of the scoundrel". On the other hand, Johnson's poet-friend Oliver Goldsmith, in his sad poem *The Deserted Village*, utters his lament over "the land, to hast'ning ills a prey, where wealth accumulates, and men decay". He looks back to the "golden age"of the past, as he remembers the village in the days of his childhood, and he vividly describes the charms of this "loveliest village of the plain"; but, he concludes, in this new, rational age, with the village deserted for the town, "all these charms are fled".

Similar, but much starker is the contrast drawn by the later poet William Blake, as he looks back to the ideal past and then forwards to the harsh reality of the present. For him the "golden age" is seen "in England's green and pleasant bowers" and in "England's pleasant pastures", to which once came "the holy Lamb of God". But now he sees, with more indignation than lamentation, "these dark Satanic mills", the new factories, that may stand for an age of reason but in opposition to the other ideal of imagination. In the past he too he looks to the ideal of "innocence", as represented by the lamb; but in the present he sees the actuality of "experience", as represented by the tiger. And among his "Songs of Experience", we find the grim description of "London" in its darker side:

I wander through each charter'd street,
Near where the chartered Thames does flow
And mark in every face I meet
Marks of weakness, marks of woe.

For him England may have become a prosperous

country, with so much emphasis on profit, based on what Shakespeare calls "inky blots and rotten parchment bonds"; but it is not a happy country. On the other hand, it was partly to get away from "the din of towns and cities", with all their weariness, partly to return to the natural scenery of his childhood, that a third poet, William Wordsworth, took the important step in 1799 of settling, with his poetic friend Samuel Coleridge, in the lovely Lake District. Till that time the Lake District had been very much "off the beaten track" and "far from the madding crowd's ignoble strife", largely untouched by the industrial or any other kind of revolution. There all was traditional and rural and charming, as it were a reversion to the childhood of man and a renewal of the "golden age". And for Wordsworth it was in fact a return to his childhood memories, as he had been born in Cockermouth on the outskirts of the District and educated at the grammar school of Hawkshead in the very midst of the District. So now he came to settle at Grasmere, near the village and beside the lake, not far from Hawkshead. It was an ideal and idyllic setting for any poet, especially a nature poet like Wordsworth; and there he became, as he calls himself, both the priest and the prophet of nature, appealing through his inspired poems to the heart of industrial England.

To the common reader, he is best known for his charming poem on the daffodils, which he saw one day in April growing "beside the lake, beneath the trees" of the nearby Ullswater. But his most representative poem, to which he gives priority over all his other poems in the collected edition of 1815, is his so-called "Immortality Ode", or (to give its longer title) his "Ode on Intimations of Immortality from Recollections of Early Childhood". Here we notice his emphasis not only on nature but also on childhood. For him the two things are not distinct but together. It is in childhood that man is closer to nature, and to God; but as he grows up, man leaves the countryside of his childhood and builds towns and cities of his own device and so cuts himself off at once from nature and from God. For, as the contemporary poet William Cowper remarked, "God made the country, and man made the town." And especially for Wordsworth, he had been close to the nature of the Lake District in his childhood; and now in his mature adulthood, after seeing for himself the ravages of the industrial revolution in England and the political revolution in France, he resolved to return both to nature and to his childhood by settling at Grasmere. In this poem, therefore, he looks back to the time, "when meadow, grove and stream, the earth, and every common sight to me did seem apparelled in celestial light, the glory and the freshness of a dream". Such is our childhood, when, he says, "heaven lies about us", as we have but recently come "from God, who is our home". But then, he adds, "shades of the prison-house begin to close upon the growing boy", till at length in manhood "the vision splendid" dies away and fades "into the light of common day".

Thus Wordsworth is not only a poet of nature, he is also nature's priest and prophet, as well as a hermit in the tradition of the desert fathers and even a friar in the Franciscan tradition. He strives to stay close to the simplicity, if not the poverty, of nature, as may be seen not only in his poems but also in his chosen dwelling in Grasmere, Dove Cottage. He aims at using the language of common life, without resorting to the sophistication of what is called "poetic diction"; and in his simple poems he celebrates simple people, such as the mysterious Lucy, who (he says) "dwelt among the untrodden ways beside the springs of Dove", as a simple "maid whom there were none to praise, and very few to love". On the other hand, the simple, rustic beauty of nature not infrequently reminds him, by contrast, of the ugliness of city life and "what Man has made of Man". Such is the continual opposition at the back of his mind and his whole life, between the "holy plan" of Nature and the sinfulness of Man as revealed in the "rationalization" of the fields and the industrialization of the towns and suburbs.

Much the same opposition is brought out, even more impressively, by Wordsworth's poetic successor, Gerard Manley Hopkins, who was in fact a priest as well as a poet. In his decision to become a Jesuit priest, well on into the reign of Queen Victoria, Hopkins effectively cut himself off from his contemporaries – no less than Wordsworth did by his decision to settle in the Lake District. And in his years of formation, as a novice at Manresa House, Roehampton, to the South-West of London, then as a student of philosophy at Stonyhurst, among the fells of Lancashire, and then as a student of theology at St. Beuno's College, in the wilds of North Wales, he may be seen as withdrawing to a pastoral life in such a "golden world" as that recalled by Shakespeare in *As You Like It*. It was indeed in the setting of what he describes as "a pastoral forehead of Wales" that he gave utterance to a new kind of poetry, with the use of what he calls "sprung rhythm" and frequent alliteration, on the occasion of a shipwreck at the mouth of the river Thames. Now after seven years of "elected silence" from the time of his entrance into the Jesuit noviceship, he composed his great masterpiece, "The Wreck of the Deutschland", "to the happy memory of five Franciscan nuns" who were drowned in the shipwreck. It may seem strange that he calls their memory "happy"; but in this new poem, he looks beyond the appearances of disaster to the reality of salvation, according to the eyes of faith. It is, he realizes, and as Shakespeare had already realized in *King Lear*, precisely misery that sees miracles; and so in the climax of the poem he sees, or the nun sees, the coming of Christ himself over the stormy waters "with a mercy that outrides the all of water".

For Hopkins, as priest and poet of nature, God is everywhere in the world, or as he himself puts it in one of his best-known poems, "The world is charged with the grandeur of God." Men may pay no attention to him, "and all is seared with trade: bleared, smeared with toil" in the new, industrial age; but Nature, on the other hand, "is never spent", rather "there lives the dearest freshness deep down things". Why? "Because," he answers, "the Holy Ghost over the bent world broods with warm breast and with ah! bright wings." Nor is it only the Holy Spirit he sees in the world, as it were in the form of a bright dove spreading its wings over the world in the clouds of sunrise. He also sees in "the azurous hung hills" on the horizon the "world-wielding shoulder" of Christ, whose glory he further recognizes "in the heavens". Yet, like Wordsworth, or even more than Wordsworth, Hopkins can't help turning with regret from the splendid world of God to the sordid world of man. Thus he draws a contrast between "the sea and the skylark" as "two noises too old to end" and the "shallow and frail town" of Rhyl, in North Wales. He describes the mediaeval beauty of Oxford, in which he finds the powers of country and town so neatly "poised" and balanced, in contrast to that "base and brickish skirt" (or outskirt) which has grown up round the recent railway station. He fondly addresses the "Earth, sweet Earth, sweet landscape" of the river Ribble, and laments the way its lovely scenery has been destroyed by the industrialist, "to his own selfbent so bound, so tied to his turn". What he sees is not only (in Wordsworth's words) "what Man has made of 'Man", but also "what Man has made of Nature"; and it is this that gives him "brows of such care, care and dear concern".

In the poetry of Hopkins as in that of Wordsworth, we find a determined "return to Nature", and through Nature, to Nature's God, but less than in Wordsworth a return to childhood – though he thought highly of the other's "Immortality Ode". Unlike the poems of Wordsworth, his work is for the most part beyond the understanding of the ordinary reader, let alone the child; but there is one poem of his, in which he aims at a Wordsworthian simplicity by addressing his words to a little girl whom he names "Margaret". It is entitled "Spring and Fall", as he imagines the little girl in the springtime of life lamenting the fall of leaves from the trees in autumn. And so he asks her, "Margaret, are you grieving over Goldengrove unleaving? Leaves, like the things of man, you with your fresh thoughts care for, can you?" It is very simple, and very charming, yet full of sadness not only over the leaves that are falling but also over the child's inevitable loss of innocence "as the heart grows older". It implies yet another contrast, as in the songs of Blake, between innocence and experience.

This yearning for the innocence of childhood, which Wordsworth did so much to evoke in the minds of his nineteenth-century readers, is everywhere apparent in the Victorian age, and in the twentieth century, too – not only in England, but throughout the world and not least in modern Japan. It appears above all in the phenomenal development during this period of children's literature, which hardly existed before but which flows like a rapidly increasing stream, fed by many torrents, from *Alice in Wonderland* by way of *Peter Rabbit* and *Winnie the Pooh* to *The Chronicles of Narnia*. It is as if a new Messianic age has dawned, in which (according to the old prophecy) the lion lies down with the lamb and (as the angel Gabriel told Zachary) the hearts of fathers are turned to their children. It was, no doubt, with this prophecy in mind that Wordsworth prefaced his "Immortality Ode" with the famous words, "The Child is father of the Man. " And Hopkins in turn drew attention to these words, by asking, "How can he be? The words are wild. Suck any sense from that who can." Yet the very fact that they are so paradoxical means that they must be true – a truth that is emphasized for twentieth-century readers by G.K. Chesterton, who dares to say of fairyland that it is "the sunny country of common sense".

10. Renaissance of Wonder

From the "enlightenment" till modern times there appears to be a straight line of development. All is so reasonable, all is so mechanical, all is so dull. Once you exclude the element of fantasy and imagination, and insist only on reason, that is the inevitable outcome: dulness. Already in the eighteenth century, the representative poet of the time, Alexander Pope, was complaining of the prevailing dulness of his contemporaries, "Thy hand, great anarch!", he exclaims to Dulness personified, "lets the curtain fall, and universal darkness buries all." Like Dr. Johnson, Pope too was a confirmed Tory, or conservative; and he deeply distrusted the governing Whig party, whom he blamed for all this dulness of the age. It was, indeed, an age when everything was sacrificed for the sake of commercial and colonial profit; and such a lust for money is, as St. Paul says, the origin of all evils – including dulness.When man forgets his eternal destiny in heaven, and seeks only his temporal advantage in this world, he can't help falling into a mood of tedium, boredom and world-weariness. As Hamlet laments, "How weary, stale, flat, and unprofitable seem to me all the uses of this world!"

All during this period, we find a prevalent dulness and seriousness at all levels of society – the aristocracy and the middle-class or bourgeoisie –except only for the lower class, who could still find humour in life, as the only way of enduring their unenviable lot. Still, in the mid-nineteenth century, we find an inevitable reaction to all this Puritan, academic seriousness, in a new "literature of nonsense", beginning with the author of the Alice books, Lewis Carroll. Already before his time there had existed in English literature a long tradition of satire, going back to the age of Shakespeare, if not before; but whereas that satire had largely been rational, the satire of this author, whose real name was Charles Lutwidge Dodgson, readily crossed the boundary dividing sense from nonsense. The very idea of "wonderland", in which Alice strays, is "dreamland", in which anything may happen. And then from the pure nonsense of this "wonderland", Lewis Carroll moves towards the more satirical nonsense of a "looking-glass" world. As an Oxford scholar at Christ Church, he satirizes what he regards as the academic nonsense of his colleagues, especially in the fields of philosophy and logic; and he reaches a climax of nonsense in his inspired poem of "Jabberwocky". Here he almost seems to be revelling in nonsense for nonsense' sake; yet he reveals something charming in all this nonsense, as it were a deeper sense, if only in the sound of words, that had been neglected by his more serious, rationalistic contemporaries.

Nor was Lewis Carroll alone in this cult of nonsense, his name is comonly associated with that of Edward Lear, the inventor of the "limerick" and to them we may add that of the great Victorian novelist, Charles Dickens, the inventor of so many memorable and humorous characters, or rather caricatures. Indeed, in these three men we may see the typical "humour" of the Victorian age, which is almost the unique contribution of England to world culture. The word, again, may be traced back to the age of Shakespeare, when it had the different meaning of a lack of balance or moderation in one's temperament – too much of one among the four "humours". But what we see in these three men is a new meaning, the readiness to perceive and enjoy the humour of life. This may well be interpreted as a reassertion of the English character against the prevailing Puritanism and science of the Victorian age, which was all too serious, solemn and dull.

They in turn may be seen as preparing the way for the emergence of the greatest genius of humour and nonsense in the history of English literature, G. K. Chesterton. From the time of his first appearance in the world of English letters, around the turn of the twentieth century, at the beginning of the new Edwardian age, he seemed like an infant prodigy among his elders, a court jester among the serious men at court, a unique man of genius who exemplified the saying, "Great wits are sure to madness near allied, and thin partitions do their bounds divide." In his younger days as an art student, he had indeed come close to madness; but he always retained sufficient sense to moderate "sense" with "nonsense". His favorite form of speech was the paradox, in which he seemed to stand the truth on its head, or rather he stood on his head in order to present the truth in an interesting manner. Thus, as we have seen, he defined "fairyland" as "the sunny country of common sense". And thus he was hailed by his contemporaries as introducing, almost single-handedly a "renaissance of wonder".

What was the meaning of this "wonder" on which Chesterton laid such emphasis in his writings – essays and poems, stories and works of literary criticism? Invariably he avoided the obvious or fashionable way of speaking, preferring rather to fly in the face of contemporary fashion. In his view, almost all the fashionable authors of his time, Wilde and Yeats, Shaw and Wells, Moore and Kipling, were what he called "heretics", individuals who spoke for their particular age against the human tradition of centuries. His ideal, which he championed against them all, was what he called "orthodoxy", not the narrow orthodoxy of his age but the universal orthodoxy of age-old tradition. Yet the way he alone defended this orthodoxy in an age of heresy, he might well be acclaimed as the champion of "paradoxy", if not of "nonsense".

A particular paradox of his appears in the title of one of his poems, "The Secret People", with its refrain, "We are the people of England, that never have spoken yet." How, we may rationally wonder, can they claim to "never have spoken yet" if they are speaking now through the mouthpiece of Chesterton? What he means, of course, is that till now they never have spoken yet, and perhaps that even now they are unable to fully express themselves.

Maybe, like Hamlet, they feel their hearts breaking, as they have to hold their tongues. All this time, from the age of Henry VIII, when there took place what Chesterton's friend Hilaire Belloc called "a revolution of the rich against the poor", the people have been silenced under a bitter oppression that has continued from that day to this. The only way they can speak, as Chesterton deeply feels, is by way of humour, of paradox, of folly, of nonsense. It is the very way Shakespeare himself chooses in his plays, in which there invariably appears the figure of fool – a fool who is in fact wiser than the seemingly wise men around him, as he is Shakespeare's own mouthpiece. Such, for instance, is the folly of Hamlet; and such, too, is the folly of King Lear. Through seeming nonsense is the way to deeper sense.

This is, indeed, a characteristically Christian way of thinking and speaking, at least from the time of St. Paul onwards. It is in his letter to the Corinthians that (as we have seen in an earlier chapter) he presents his ideal of "wise folly", which is based on the folly of the cross. Jesus himself may have spoken words of wisdom but his whole life, and especially his death, is folly in the eyes of this world; and so to receive his words and to base our lives on them, we have need of the folly of Christ. From then onwards we may trace a line of holy men who have been "perfect fools" for Christ's sake, as we see in the lives of many desert fathers and not least of St. Francis of Assisi. Even the founder of the Society of Jesus, St.Ignatius, who seems so prudent and reserved in contrast to St. Francis, set it down as a basic rule for his followers (including Gerard Manley Hopkins and myself) that they should be willing to be regarded as fools for the sake of Christ.

Such is the secret behind the "renaissance of wonder" brought about by Chesterton. After all, a person who is filled with wonder often seems a fool in the eyes of others who fail to understand the reason of his wonder. Or at least, he seems little better than a child, lacking in the responsibility or maturity of an adult. On the other hand, as he doesn't mind being regarded or even despised as a fool or a child, he is free to say what he likes, according to the traditional license granted to fools and children; and then very often what he says touches, if not the conscious minds, at least the sub-conscious hearts of his hearers or readers. Moreover, with this freedom, a gate of inspiration is opened to him that is usually closed to men of a more serious cast of mind. When we are under the impression that everything we say has to be thoroughly reasonable, or else it is subject to rational criticism, we have to be very careful in all we say, and this thought prevents us from saying much we would like to say or even from thinking of what we might say. And because Chesterton is swayed less by conscious reason, according to the old-fashioned ideal of the "enlightenment", than by his sub-conscious inspiration, no wonder he comes out with so many wonderful sayings that gave rise to this "renaissance of wonder".

But, we may ask, hasn't any other author arisen to take up his prophet's cloak to continue and consolidate this renaissance? I can name at least two well-known authors of recent times, who both happened to be teachers of mine in the School of English at Oxford University. One was the Protestant apologist, C.S.Lewis, who stood out in the post-war years, like Chesterton, both as a modern champion of Christianity and as an imaginative teller of tales for children with his *Chronicles of Narnia*. The other was the Catholic scholar, J.R.R. Tolkien, who never wrote in defence of Christianity, though he was always a devout Catholic, but who revealed an even more fertile imagination in his *Lord of the Rings*. They are the two best-selling Christian authors today; and through their imaginative writings they show their young readers a wholly new way of looking at the world – the way not of scientific reason but of poetic imagination.

It would be wrong, however, to think of their imagination as entirely fantastic, or idiotic, personal to themselves. Even more than Chesterton, both Lewis and Tolkien look for the source of their creative imagination to the Christian Middle Ages away from the rationalistic "enlightenment" of more recent times. They were both mediaeval scholars and could well enter into the mind of their seemingly remote period. That was an age the human imagination flourished, by the side of the human intellect, as it were under the divine blessing; but with the rise of science in the seventeenth century, all the emphasis was laid on the human reason (on a lower level than the human intellect), while that reason was directed more to things of earth than to things of heaven. And so it was necessary for them, as it had been to the romantic poets in the age of Wordsworth, to look back to the earlier period for their new inspiration.

11. Approach to Ecology

Now at last we come to the present age, at the end of the twentieth century. Now, in spite of all our vaunted scientific progress, two world wars separate us from the peaceful, prosperous age of Edwardian England. And not only two world wars, but all kinds of other lesser wars and greater horrors in the name of "ethnic cleansing". Even in peace there have taken place all kinds of economic calamities and atrocities committed as well against the defenceless poor as against the equally defenceless plants and animals on the face of our planet. All this has been made possible by the advance of science and technology, the latest fruits of the mythical tree of knowledge that have now come to seem more evil than good – real evil and only apparent good. Thus we have come to face the related problems of destitution and starvation in the countries of the third world and the denudation of the tropical forests, with their frightening global consequences for all alike, rich as well as poor, first as well as third world. And thus the boasted "reason" of the enlightenment and the rise of science has come to be shown up in the long run as a form of madness, or what T.S.Eliot calls "merely a receipt for deceit", merely a "knowledge of dead secrets" or secrets that lead by way of power over nature to self destruction.

It is significant that at the beginning of this long period of development, in the sixteenth century, there appears the story of Faust – set in Luther's university town of Wittenberg – in which the hero is shown as selling his soul to the devil in return for knowledge and power. It is also, implicitly, the story of Shakespeare's Macbeth, who similarly gives his "eternal jewel ... to the common enemy of man" in return for sovereign power, only to find himself deceived by the bargain, and to find that such sovereign power, which had before seemed so splendid to his eyes, is in reality "full of sound and fury, signifying nothing". It is the opening of his eyes to his real nakedness, such as

Adam first experienced in the Garden of Eden after having eaten the fruit of the forbidden tree of knowledge. And now in our modern age we are experiencing the same opening of our eyes to the same nakedness, only on a larger scale than ever before. For it is a nakedness that affects not only men and women on earth, but the earth itself, as it is progressively denuded of plants and trees by the skill of scientific technology, and the very atmosphere round the earth. In our "accursed thirst for gold" we are hastening blindly to take destruction of ourselves and our planet. And so the end of the world, prophesied in the scriptures, is about to be realized at the hands not of an avenging God but of greedy mankind.

What can we do, we ask, to avoid this impending calamity? What has been done at the highest levels, by politicians and scientists as well as a few environmentalists, at the recent Earth Summit at Rio de Janeiro? Well, they talk and talk in endless discussions, and the minutes of those discussions are duly recorded on reams and reams of paper (serving only to denude the rain forests even more rapidly). Then, large sums of money are allocated to scientific and political institutes for further investigation of the problem and examination of the atmosphere over the earth. Meanwhile, the problem of the environment, like the parallel problem of Bosnia, becomes ever more serious, and there is no end in sight. As for ordinary people like ourselves, who constitute the vast majority of the human race, we feel there is nothing we can do personally about so vast a problem; and so we do nothing about it, or if anything, we aggravate it as we have been doing, all unconsciously, all along.

When we honestly reflect on the problem and its causes, we have to admit that we are not merely helpless victims of the situation, but also guilty villains. It is not only the scientists and the politicians behind them who have brought about this lamentable state of affairs, but all of us who have somehow abetted and profited from what the scientists and the politicians have done over the past three centuries or so. The original sin has been committed not just by a few men in prominent positions, with knowledge and power, but by all men, or rather by Man which is the original meaning, in Hebrew, of the name of Adam. We have all sinned, and we are all in need of salvation. But from where may we expect that salvation to come? Are we merely to expect it, without doing anything. Or is there anything we can do about it, to bring it about for ourselves and others, and for the earth on which we live?

It seems to me that there is much we can do about the problem, without waiting for the politicians and the scientists to solve it for us – if they ever do or can solve it. When we look more deeply into the problem, in the light of its origins some time towards the beginning of the seventeenth century, we find that it came about not only from the desire of knowledge and power, but also from a mistaken presupposition behind that desire. What is it? It is to be found, I submit, in the wrong interpretation of Genesis, where God blesses Adam and Eve and allows them to subdue the earth, and "subdue" is taken to mean "exploit the resources without limit". It was the false presupposition of Bacon and his followers that there need be no limit either to knowledge or to power, either to our exploration of nature's secrets or to our exploitation of earth's resources. And behind that false presupposition was the equally false presupposition that man with his reason is somehow set apart from nature on the face of the earth, to use it as he pleases without being in any way indebted to it. This is what T.S. Eliot has quaintly called, with reference to the poetry of the seventeenth century, "a dissociation of sensibility" – or a separation of feeling from reason. It leads directly to the accusation of "pathetic fallacy" against those who cling, somewhat sentimentally, to the original association of man with plants and animals. It is againstthis accusation that Wordsworth asserts his faith "that every flower enjoys the air it breathes", while he grieves over "what Man has made of Man".

Here is, it seems to me, at least the hint of a solution to the problem. For if the problem arises out of an undue desire for knowledge and power, a knowledge and a power that regards "the other" (outside the human self) as "object", the solution has to be found in love, a love that embraces all things and persons as one. Scientific knowledge regards all things, even including other human beings, as objects, to be studied with dispassionate, non-judgmental, academic objectivity. But love, especially as found in poets and children, regards all things, whether animals or plants or even stones, as endowed with personality, at least in view of their creation by a God of love. In the view of love, there can be no "pathetic fallacy", but the only fallacy lies in the accusation of "pathetic fallacy". For behind that accusation is the presupposition of a separation between man with his reason and other creatures, which is a denial of love. Rather, as Shakespeare rightly affirms, "Love hath reason, reason none." It is the paradox that there is more reason in love than in reason itself; or rather, that in love we come close to the wisdom of God, from which we turn away by our undue emphasis on the conscious reason of man. As Bacon himself realized, though his followers often failed to realize it, "a little philosophy [such as one finds in experimental science] inclineth man's mind to atheism". Such philosophy is that which is given by the tree of knowledge; but there is a higher, and deeper, philosophy provided by the other, tree of life, namely, the philosophy of love.

Such a love I find already expressed by Shakespeare's poet-king, Richard II, on his return to English soil from his wars in Ireland. "Dear earth," he exclaims, exuding poetic sentiment, "I do salute thee with my hand." He even compares himself with this earth to "a long-parted mother with her child", as she "plays fondly with her tears and smiles in meeting". He may not be an ideal king in his all too tyrannical treatment of his subjects, and so he is

90

deservedly deposed; but he seems to me ideal in his poetic sentiment towards the earth. The same sentiment is later expressed by the Victorian poet, Gerard Manley Hopkins, in his above-mentioned poem, *Ribblesdale*, which he opens by fondly addressing the "Earth, sweet Earth, sweet landscape", in the very spirit of Shakespeare's poet-king. He imagines the earth appealing from the obstinate wickedness of man to heaven, "with no tongue to plead, no heart to feel", yet making her strong plea by merely being and suffering – besides using the words of the poet as "Earth's eye, tongue, or heart". Again, in his Oxford poem on "Binsey Poplars" he tenderly speaks of "My aspens dear", lamenting that they are "all felled, felled, are all felled", in the very accents of Shakespeare's Macduff, lamenting the murder of his wife and children, "All my pretty ones? Did you say all? O hell-kite! All? What!All my pretty chickens and their dam at one fell swoop?"

Here precisely is the deep meaning of the "return to nature" advocated by the Stoics, and the "return to childhood" advocated by Christ as well as by Wordsworth. It is, after all, only natural to children, as we see by daily experience, to see themselves as close to animals and animals as close to them; and they often treat plants and even stones in the same way. And nowadays it is not uncommon for ordinary men and women, with the approval and encouragement of biologists, to have pet plants and pet rocks and even to talk to them and show affection for them. This may seem nothing but an amiable eccentricity, to be indulged but hardly to be commended. Yet it seems to indicate a way of closing the unnatural gap that has been made since the seventeenth century by thinkers like Bacon and Descartes, with their excessive emphasis on pure reason. Even before their time, of course, men didn't speak so much to plants or animals; and the vast majority of human discourse is among human beings. Yet even in the Bible, we find the last instruction of Jesus to his disciples, to go "into all the world and preach the Gospel to every creature" – an instruction that seems to have been taken literally by St. Francis in preaching to the birds, and by St. Anthony in preaching to the fishes. There, too, we also find the words of St. Paul to the Romans about the whole creation groaning in the pains as of childbirth, and waiting for the manifestation of the sons of God. And today such groaning is all too audible from all sides, from animals as they are slaughtered for meat, from the trees as they are cut down for man's various needs, and from man himself as he suffers at the hands of his fellow-men. All men are villains, and yet now we see all men as victims. And all alike, men and animals and plants and the earth as a whole, are awaiting salvation, or what St. Paul calls "the manifestation of the sons of God".

Not that I am all together in favour of what I have just called "amiable eccentricity": I only mention it as a hint of a solution. Rather, what is important as a means of solving the vast environmental problem, a means that is open to everyone, is for us to pay more attention to and show greater appreciation for all God's creatures. Here, too, we may learn much from the poetry of Hopkins, as when in "The Wreck of the Deutschland" he kisses his hand "to the stars, lovely-asunder starlight, not because he is in love with the stars themselves, personified as pretty girls, but because they seem to waft the splendour of God out of their starlight, and he is primarily in love with God. This is precisely the attitude we find everywhere in the Bible and in the writings of the saints towards the works of salvation. There creation is shown in its essential relation to the Creator; and when the works of creation are admired, as in the lovely Psalm 104, they are admired not so much for themselves as for their great Creator. "Bless the Lord, my soul!" exclaims the Psalmist. "O Lord, my God, you are very great. You are clothed with honour and majesty. You cover yourself with light as with a garment. You stretch out the heavens like a curtain."

This is precisely the solution I have in mind. For the

problem is not just one derived from the desire for knowledge or power, but one consisting in disobedience to God, and forgetfulness of his grandeur. When Eve was enticed by the serpent, according to the story of Genesis, to take the fruit of the forbidden tree, her sin and the consequent sin of Adam consisted not so much in taking the fruit as in doing what was forbidden. In other words, they sought a knowledge of things apart from their due submission to God; but, as they soon came to realize, things without God, or creatures without their Creator, are next to nothing. After all, it was by the divine Word in the beginning that they were all drawn out of nothing. And so, when they are seen and admired and appreciated not in themselves but in relation to their Creator, as objects of praise and gratitude to God, then they are truly known. And therein lies the difference between the wisdom of the ancients, who were content to contemplate the world and to praise God for all they saw in the world, and the knowledge of the moderns, who must needs go on from knowledge to power, to the use and abuse of the world. The former wisdom is the way of life; but the latter knowledge is the way of death.

About the Author

Peter Milward was born in London in 1925, studied at Wimbledon College 1933-43, entered the Society of Jesus 1943, studied philosophy at Heythrop College, Oxon. 1947-50, classical and English literature at Campion Hall, Oxford, 1950-54, moved to Japan in 1954, studied Japanese, then theology at St. Mary's college, Tokyo (faculty of theology, Sophia University), 1955-61, was ordained priest 1960, began teaching in the department of English Literature, Sophia University, 1962. Specializing in Shakespearian drama, he published his first book, *An Introduction to Shakespeare's Plays*, 1964, followed by *Christian Themes in English Literature*, 1967. After further research at the Shakespeare Institute, Birmingham, 1965-66, he published *Shakespeare's Religious Background*, 1973; and as a result of subsequent research at the Huntington Library, Calfornia, he went on to publish two volumes of *Religious Contoversies of the Elizabethan Age* and *the Jacobean Age* in 1977 and 1978. Besides being vice-chairman of the Renaissance Institute of Sophia University, he is editor of "Renaissance Monographs" and of the Japanese *Renaissance Sōsho*; and with the opening of the Renaissance Centre in the new library of Sophia University in 1984, he was appointed its first director. He has also published books on Gerard Manley Hopkins and T.S. Eliot, as well as many volumes of essays for Japanese students.